Fins de Siècle

Parallax 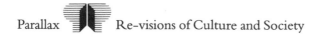 Re-visions of Culture and Society

STEPHEN G. NICHOLS, GERALD PRINCE, AND WENDY STEINER,
SERIES EDITORS

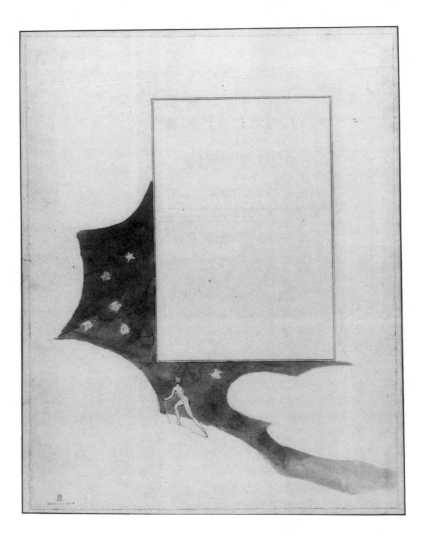

William Blake. Watercolor illustration for Edward Young's Night Thoughts.
Verso of title page. 1796. British Museum, London.

Fins de Siècle

English Poetry in
1590, 1690, 1790, 1890, 1990

Edited by

ELAINE SCARRY

The Johns Hopkins University Press

Baltimore and London

The Johns Hopkins University Press
2715 North Charles Street
Baltimore, Maryland 21218-4319
The Johns Hopkins Press Ltd., London

Library of Congress Cataloging-in-Publication Data
will be found at the end of this book.
A catalog record for this book is available from the British Library.

ISBN 0-8018-4928-4
ISBN 0-8018-4929-2 (pbk.)

Contents

Preface

꙰

*T*HE CHAPTERS in *Fins de Siècle* describe the ways the approaching end of a century can affect and reshape the poetic forms of a given era. In the 1590s there suddenly appears in England the genre of the sonnet sequence, which, in its exhausted, repetitive, unending display of vir-tuosity—as Margreta de Grazia argues—seems (like the century itself) uncertain of its ability to end. The odes and masques of the 1690s, according to Leo Braudy, not only participate in, but at times direct, the decisive political shift toward greater distribution: these poems record the end-of-century turn from monarchy to social contract, from court to representative assembly, from limited privilege to univer-sal rights. They also designate the poet, rather than the monarch, as the center of cultural authority and, in doing so, make "the aesthetic" a new center of power available to all within the population who seek it. For Jerome McGann, the impact of the 1790s on the structure of sentimental lyric is again strong: all that is implied by the term *fin-de-siècle decadence*—lassitude, eros, artifice, literalism—suddenly erupts in the Della Cruscan movement, which in turn deeply marks romantic poetry, either as a positive influence (on Blake and Coleridge in the 1790s; on Byron, Shelley, and Keats later) or by providing the poetic practice against which they reacted (as it did for Wordsworth, whose revolutionary aesthetic announced in the 1800 "Preface" to the *Lyrical Ballads* is a direct response to the Della Cruscans). The two possibilities always available in a century's final decade—sensuous exhaustion or instead an originary, inaugural attempt to endow the coming century with new tools—are thus brought face to face in this vivid standoff

ix

where, McGann argues, they come to occupy a single ground. The lyric of the 1890s, in Helen Vendler's account, is incandescently aware that its own brevity and immediacy place it at odds with the epic sweep of history and hence with any easy registration of the fin de siècle. Yet it discovers brilliant ways to fit into the small compass of its own utterance the calendric fatality that stretches along the poet's horizon. The metaphysical solutions created by Yeats in the 1890s shaped his later poems (as well as much of our own thinking) once the century turned. But now, "the century clicking by," those solutions are unavailable to the poets of the 1990s who, like Jorie Graham, situate themselves "deep into the lateness now," to discover new ways of folding history into lyric in order to provide the linguistic endowments of a future time.

It is an odd—perhaps even an extraordinary—fact that many major poets wrote in final decades: Dante, for example, wrote *Vita Nuova* in 1294 and situated the *Divine Comedy* in the year 1300; Chaucer wrote most of the *Canterbury Tales* in the 1390s; Shakespeare wrote the sonnets and twenty-two of the plays in the 1590s, the decade in which Spenser's *Epithalamion* and *Faerie Queene* also appeared. If one were to assume, for a moment, that this outcome is not sheer coincidence, what explanation might account for it? What would an explanation even sound like? My own essay puts forward a speculative answer: I argue that it is the place of numbers within poetry and poetry's address to problems of agency that make it so responsive to turns in the calendar.

Each of the chapters in this book is centrally about the calendar. Margreta de Grazia gives a vivid portrait of the impact of the 1590s on poetry, especially the sonnet ("from *sonnetto*, or 'small sound' "). Yet she requires us to set this (in itself wholly convincing) account against a second, very different ribbon of argument in which "fin de siècle" does not even begin until two centuries later. A third ribbon of her argument theorizes about the nature of periodization in both the past and the present, including the startling way in which calendric units eventually begin to acquire human characteristics. Her rigorous interrogation of temporal words and phrases—"sequence," "century," "millennia," "*Anno Domini*," "time out of mind"—is periodically interrupted by strangely tender imaginings of the fin de siècle as an

Olympic runner racing toward a line of demarcation, or as an Hegelian reader, curled up in a chair, wishing to exempt itself from the rest of its century.

The mysteries of periodization also preoccupy Leo Braudy in his "Missing Decade of the 1690s." How can it be that the 1690s exist only as a hole or tear in the calendar? Ordinarily, the list of climactic final decades includes the 1590s, the 1790s, and the 1890s, and pointedly excludes the 1690s. The decade is even "missing" in the calendric picture of the seventeenth and eighteenth centuries, where it is squeezed out between the terms "Restoration" and "Augustan," the one (as Braudy writes) ballooning forward, the other ballooning back. This disappearance is especially odd since it is during this period that the calendar itself, along with many other cultural and political instruments, ceases to be dynastic property and comes to be perceived as belonging to the population at large. Braudy gives a richly detailed account of this decisive decade: far from "summarizing" the previous century, it became the "tabula rasa" for the future, setting in place constitutionalism, feminism, and the model of the state that would be "imitated and extended" in the revolutions at the end of the next century.

Given the scale of the legacy of the 1690s, it is not surprising that some of the lineaments of the decade should reappear in the picture of the 1790s drawn by Jerome McGann: the particular conception of the sensate mind in the writings of John Locke passes in the eighteenth century through Lawrence Sterne into the fin-de-siècle poetry of the Della Cruscans; so too the aesthetic and political pluralism of that earlier final decade now returns in the Della Cruscan emphasis on the equality of male and female voices. For the Della Cruscans, the major form of song is the *tenso*, and the "defining event" is the kiss. The tenso, the form of poetry that had been the vehicle of all-male debate among twelfth-century troubadours, now becomes the vehicle of a fervently heterosexual poetic exchange. The kiss comes to summarize "art's capacity to deal with fatal circumstance."

Fins de Siècle closes, as it opens, with explicit attention to the problem of periodization. "Matters of such gravity as how to demarcate time," writes Helen Vendler, "are not solved, of course, in lyric; they are merely reimagined." Among the many features that differentiate the 1890s from the 1990s—the one decade "weary" and the other "confused"; the one "painting static" and the other "screen mobile"; the one "declarative" and the other "interrogative"—perhaps the most striking is the distance between the decisive forms of temporal demarcation in the first, and the self-conscious reluctance to demarcate in the second. Yeats introduces into his poems a sequence of calendric shapes and lines—circular, straight, rising and falling—that follow from his four models of history (the "classical, Christian, Celtic, and Nietzschean"). None of these are found in Jorie Graham's poems, where one finds instead self-conscious meditation on the "recording of time" and exquisite hesitation about arbitrary acts of line making.

In Jorie Graham's "century clicking by," Helen Vendler puts before us a new situation. Writers such as Paul Fussell and Frank Kermode have called attention to the extraordinary acoustical magic by which we unselfconsciously convert—at least we used to do so in the past—an unbroken sameness of sound, tick-tick-tick-tick, into the rhythmically complete pairings tick-tock, tick-tock, each with its tidy opening and close ("tick is a humble genesis, tock a feeble apocalypse," writes Kermode). If we now willfully abstain from even this elementary form of demarcation, we abstain from much more, since the perception of beginning and end lies beneath many other narrative and historical patterns.

Of course, it is not just our own century, but every century, that must end without assistance from the past, for as this book makes clear, each fin de siècle tends to be proleptic, precocious of a future time: the 2000-year cycle that we might expect to be appropriate to the 1990s was already richly imagined by Yeats, the poet whose mental life was shaped by the 1890s; in turn, the erotic decadence we often locate in the 1890s was already the verbal practice of the Della Cruscans in the 1790s; the revolutionary spirit at the heart of the 1790s was elaborately prepared for by the generous political remappings of the 1690s; even the "missing" decade of the 1690s can be backdated to the 1590s, for we are asked in this book to imagine omitting it from the sequence of final decades. Still, all precocity aside, the very self-consciousness of the 1990s ensures that our own turn will entail the consultation of many earlier models.

"This is what we call making an exit," says Clove in Samuel Beckett's *Endgame*. *Fins de Siècle* is a small handbook on how to make an exit: the farewell kiss of the Della Cruscans; the Hegelian reader exempting itself from the rest of its century; the Renaissance sonnet sequence simply refusing to end; the panicked bird of Jorie Graham that flies into a room and cannot find the doorway out. Centuries are turned with the help of poets, and the poetic voice that crosses the line of demarcation tends always to be a specific one, whether the sonnet ("small sound") of the 1590s, the masque of the 1690s, the tenso of the 1790s, or the lyric of the 1890s. These pictures from the past also work to make more acute our attention to the poetic voice of the present final decade, the acoustical signature of our own century's turn.

Fins de Siècle

Introduction

✿✿✿

Counting at Dusk
(Why Poetry Matters When the Century Ends)

Elaine Scarry

*W*HY SHOULD the end of a century mark poetry so deeply? Why should it in particular mark lyric so deeply? There are strong reasons why it should *not* mark it at all, since, as Helen Vendler writes, the subject is "unsuitable" to lyric: fin de siècle "derives from the time span of epic narration, and lyric generically prefers the moment to the narrative span." But not only is it marked: its being marked is awaited, expected. "The world is waiting for the poet," Allen Grossman keeps telling us in the late twentieth century. If the mounting number of poetry readings in the 1990s is indicative, the world is, if not waiting for the poet, at least newly alert to its need for poetry. This seems true of other final decades. "Is any new poetry in the wind?" Thomas Hardy suddenly asks in the last line of the last letter he wrote in the winter of 1899.[1] And Wordsworth in the 1790s openly sets out at once to incite and to fulfil the expectation for the new: his poems, he repeatedly presses in the "Preface" to the *Lyrical Ballads,* are "an experiment"; they are "materially different from those upon which general approbation is at present bestowed"; they differ from "the popular Poetry of the day";[2] he is creating something original and therefore has "the task of *creating* the taste by which he is to be enjoyed"; he is called upon both "to clear and often to shape his own road."[3]

I

Why poetic practice should be so marked is partially explained by what happens in the wake of numbers. But it is also in part explained by the direct experience of numbers themselves. Mathematicians have described the acute pleasure they take in the practice of their trade and have likened it to certain forms of aesthetic pleasure. Solving the proof for the square root of 2, writes Seymour Papert, entails the delight of watching the numeral 2 flit from side to side across the equal sign, now appearing as a number, now disappearing and returning as a super-script: the process bears a strong resemblance, he says, to the pleasure one feels at a theatrical play, with its rhythm of entrances and exits, its disappearances and unforeseen returns.[4]

Even the simpler and more widely practiced sequence of counting has this drama. The numbers mount (6, 7, 8, 9), then suddenly disap-pear into a nullity (0), which brings an alteration in the next column (10), introducing numerical activity in a place where there had been none before. It is as though the sequence of units suddenly becomes a lever able to act on the space adjacent to itself, shifting the location of drama from its own habitually perturbed territory to its normally un-disturbed neighbor. The ones column is so hyperactive that it hardly occasions attention. Activity in the tens column brings notice: when it is one's own age (30, 40, 50, 60), it may even be treated as a grand event. The hundreds column is still more portentous: objects of every color are priced at \$4.99 or \$499 not because anyone fails to see that one more unit will affect the hundreds column but precisely because everyone sees that one more unit will affect the hundreds column. We accept it as a legitimate display of restraint: our merchant-guardians have prohibited numerical activity from straying recklessly into the next column (\$5.00, \$500). The sudden disturbance in the hundreds or the thousands column—1699 to 1700, 1799 to 1800, 1899 to 1900, 1999 to 2000—brings a slight thrill even when it is only occurring on an odometer, even, that is, when it involves only one's own solitary encapsulated vehicle. How much more so when it is a calendar: it is as though here and there all over the world, everyone with their widely divergent genre of vehicles (horseback, muleback, camelback, car-riage), their different road surfaces (tarmac, sand, water), their habits of motion, were simultaneously, despite their prior unmindfulness of one another, to look down at the odometer strapped to their ankle, or bike handle, or car, and see that it was about to turn from 1999 to 2000 and know that in many places elsewhere everyone had reached the same interval. (The numerical would temporarily cease to be a background calibration but would seem instead the point of arrival, the destination toward which everyone had all along been heading.) This experience—happening just as one started up a long hill, just as another arrived at a son's wedding, just as another practiced a new song, just as another crossed Simplon Pass, just as another rushed to be beside someone injured, just as another wondered if the odometer was working—would seem highly particularized and intimate yet would carry the vertigo of collective fate normally occasioned only by earth-imperiling or -saving events. Thus even if the new century properly begins in 2001, part of the deep experiential turn will come in 1999 and the interim year 2000.

If one were to say, "Many people will notice this numerical change," should one add, "Even poets," or should one instead say, "Especially poets"?

Counting has its own cadence; cadence imposes the constraint of counting. So does lineation. Thus the names of poetic forms are persistently numerical—couplets, quatrains, terza rima, octave, sestet, sestina, ottava rima, iambic pentameter, hexameter, triolet—because the poetic voice seldom ceases to count. At the end of the century, verse may become explicitly calendric. Set in the jubilee year 1300, Dante's *Divine Comedy* has 100 cantos.[5] Composed in 1595, Spenser's *Epithalamion* has 24 stanzas and 365 long lines.[6] Shakespeare's sonnets of the 1590s, Margreta de Grazia persuasively shows, present themselves as a book of hours. Written in 1594, *Romeo and Juliet* absorbs into its structure what Walter Pater sees as a heightened form of the nocturne.[7] But quite apart from the ends of the century, poetry is deeply calendric. Pater, for example, calls attention to the way the nocturne of Provençal poetry is always subdivided according to the hour at which it was to be sung ("Some were to be sung at midnight—songs inviting to sleep, the *serena*, or *serenade*; others at break of day—waking songs, the *aube*, or *aubade*"), just as Spenser urged that the eclogue was always a genre devoted to the calendar year; and even without these recognizable temporal names (day, night, week, month, year) poetry has in common with the calendar the unceasing act of numerical counting.

In any sonnet, in other words, regardless of the decade, the iambs, the pentameter line, the octave and the sestet establish at its interior a calendric sequence of moments and hours, its inevitable daybreak, its anticipated nightfall. The point is not, then, that poetry *becomes* numerical at the fin de siècle. Exactly the reverse: it is the very persistence of the act of counting, its ongoing inseparability from the poetic act, which ensures that this external event in the realm of counting—the turning over of the calendar—is likely to be noticed. For a person with high numerical sensitivity, any activity in the hundreds column is likely to be perceived not as an abstract experience but as something occurring in one's own interior. Hardy said, for example, that the shift from the nineteenth to the twentieth century changed the way the words of a song felt in his mouth and the way coins weighed in his hands.[8] For Coleridge, similarly, the turn from 1799 to 1800 registered itself in the intimate space between fingertips and eyes: "How many Thousand Letter-writers," he wrote to William Godwin in early January, "will in the first fortnight of this month write a 7 first, & then transmogrify it into an 8—in the dates of their Letters! I like to catch myself doing that which involves any identity of the human Race."[9] In each case the calendar binds the intimate to the collective: the song in Hardy's mouth was the national anthem; Coleridge saw in the conversion of his 7s into 8s the numerical rehabilitation of the whole species.

The etymological identity of *meter* with *measure,* the intimacy between poetry and the act of counting, and hence the heightened poetic attention to numbers at the moment when the calendar turns over are vividly illustrated in Wordsworth's extraordinary last letter of 1799. Written to Coleridge on December 24 and December 27, it provides an account of the arrival of Wordsworth and his sister Dorothy at their Grasmere cottage, their rapid attempts to domesticate and inhabit it (clearing away smoke, learning the flues, making curtains), their plans for building an enclosed garden in the summer, and then, most elaborately, a detailed description of their four-day winter journey that had brought them to this cottage, from Sockburn to Grasmere, at least forty-five miles of it on foot, occasionally supplemented for small intervals by horses, pony carts, and a post chaise.[10] Perhaps not surprisingly, the letter is a stunning piece of description: moonlight falling on snow-covered meadows on their first morning; the orange light of the second dawn reflected in a brook in an otherwise dark valley, the brightness of the orange brook "varying according to the agitation of the current"; their eventual climb over "stones of all colours . . . encased in the clearest ice" to arrive beneath the vaulted "cieling of a huge cave" where a powerful stream of water hurls rocks before falling into a spray of dissolving snow, the intricate secret interior of "this Arabian scene" seeming in its cascading details to anticipate the not-yet-dreamed dream of Kubla Khan. The letter documents with exquisite precision the sensory perceptions of the present (a "keen frosty morning," a succession of light snowfalls on their faces and backs, their numb feet aching with cold during the last two miles of "hard frozen road" on the first day's walk, his sister's "raging toothache" as she later sits sewing the cottage curtains). Yet it continually trips the calendar forward. The Grasmere cottage already has, at least in speculative form, the small enclosed garden that they would later make in the summer of 1800 and fill with honeysuckle, roses, and the red blossoms of runner bean vines.[11] So, too, key locations in the Sockburn-Grasmere walk are continually tripped forward out of the winter of 1799 into the summer of the 1800s (detouring in one case through an earlier fin de siècle). Of the waterfall they see at sunset on the first day he writes: "such a performance as you might have expected from some giant gardiner employed by one of Queen Elizabeth's Courtiers, if this same giant gardiner had consulted with Spenser and they two had finish'd the work together." And his long description of the huge cave entered on the second day climaxes once more into a garden, compressing into itself "all that summer and winter can produce of delicate beauty":

> The rock in the centre of these falls where the water was most abundant, deep black, the adjoining parts yellow white purple violet and dove colour'd, or covered with water-plants of the most vivid green, and hung with streams and fountains of ice and icicles that in some places seemed to conceal the verdure of the plants and the variegated colours of the rocks and in some places to render their hues more splendid. I cannot express to you the enchanted effect produced by this Arabian scene of colour as the wind blew aside the great waterfall behind which we stood and hid and revealed each of these faery cataracts in irregular succession or displayed

them with various gradations of distinctness, as the intervening spray was thickened or dispersed. In the luxury of our imaginations we could not help feeding on the pleasure which in the heat of a July noon this cavern would spread through a frame exquisitely sensible.[12]

As the Grasmere garden and orchard are glimpsed through the curtained smoke of the troublesome winter chimneys, so here again the 1800s' first July is half displayed, half concealed in the curtain of waters.

Yet this conflation of the delicate and the miraculous is steadily paced, for Wordsworth periodically erupts into the prosaic act (or actually, the poetic act) of counting: 12 miles on foot on day 1, 3 of those in the dark, 2 of those with hurt feet; 21 miles on day 2, occurring in segments of ¼ mile, 1½ miles, 2 miles (the distance traveled with the help of the ponies and carts), 10 miles in 2¼ hours, 7 miles in 1 hour 35 minutes; on day 3, 11 miles in 3 hours. Periods of rest are measured as well: 1 hour at the domed cave; ¼ hour "close by Garsdale chapel." Even the landscape structures itself into countable objects: 2 fields, 2 banks, 2 rocky banks, 1st waterfall, 2d waterfall, 3d waterfall (its "water fell at least ten yards from us"), 2 winding rocky banks, 3 festoons embedded in the rock, 3 diminutive waterfalls near the 3d large waterfall. He performs throughout the letter a dedicated labor of measurement: it is as though he were to speak aloud the poetry of *An Evening Walk* (1793) or *Descriptive Sketches* (1793) but periodically break from its language into a vocalization of the stress counts, alternating between phrases and numbers the way dancers in the rigor of training sometimes count aloud.

The fin de siècle has been, over a sequence of centuries, devoted to the aesthetic, not just to poetry but to literature more broadly, and not just to literature but to music and to the visual arts. William Godwin, for example, said that 1799–1800 marked "a great epocha, or division in [his] life" because it was at that moment that he "began to read [not poetry but more inclusively] the old English authors."[13] The 1690s were dedicated, as Leo Braudy makes clear, not just to poetry but to sentimental drama. The 1590s saw not just the sudden proliferation of sonnet sequences but also the less overtly lyric genres of epigram and satire, neatly trimmed to fit the period: "A crackdown in censorship [in 1599] which called for the banning and burning of satirical works," writes Margreta de Grazia, "[brought] the genre to an abrupt halt." Still, while other genres have flourished at the centuries' turn, it is also the case that some, such as drama, have done so by absorbing poetry into their own lineaments: Austin Clarke, for example, points out that the drama of the 1590s (Shakespeare's comedies and histories), the 1790s (the five-act blank-verse tragedies of Coleridge, Wordsworth, and later, Byron and Shelley), and the 1890s (Yeats' many verse plays, Hardy's 125-scene *Dynasts*) has consistently been dedicated to poetic theater.[14] Perhaps more to the point, since at least the 1390s, when Chaucer wrote the *Canterbury Tales* (most tales between 1392 and 1395; several, such as the Nun's Priest's Tale, between 1396 and 1400),[15] final decades have produced a legacy of poets—Chaucer, Spenser, Shakespeare, Donne, Dryden, Blake, Coleridge, Wordsworth, Hardy, Yeats—who cannot, by any method of counting, be calculated as one-tenth of the calendar's cut. In many of these cases, the poet's major work appeared during the nineties or at the century's turn: Chaucer's *Canterbury Tales,* Spenser's *Faerie Queene* and *Epithalamion,* Shakespeare's sonnets and twenty-two of the plays, many of Donne's songs and sonnets, Blake's *Songs of Innocence and Experience* as well as many of the prophetic books, the *Lyrical Ballads* of Wordsworth and Coleridge. In other instances, the nineties have had a decisive impact on the poetry even when the poems themselves were written over several decades: it is in the 1890s, for example, that Hardy suddenly gives up novel writing and dedicates himself to poetry, a dedication from which he then never swerved. Yeats' major poems, though not written in the 1890s, are—as Helen Vendler shows—themselves re-writings of his earlier fin-de-siècle lyrics.

Special pleading for the primacy of poetry at the ends of centuries does not seem wholly out of place because it has often been during these very periods that such special pleading has itself taken place. In 1595, Sidney's *Defence of Poesy* was published,[16] placing poetry above the other arts, as well as above philosophy and history. In 1694, Dryden asserted the primacy of poetry over painting (poems were there in the Garden; painting came after the Fall) in a poem written to a painter.[17] In his dedication to his translation of Vergil's *Aeneid,* also written in 1694, the poem is superior not only to painting but to all other human outcomes: "An Heroic Poem, truly such, is undoubtedly the greatest Work which the Soul of Man is capable to perform."[18] For Dryden, the poet displaces not just the painter and other artists but, as Leo Braudy so crucially shows, the monarch as a site of cultural authority.[19] Whereas access to the monarchy is limited to inheritance, access to poetry is achievable through education and "taste"; hence it is distributed to an ever widening population. The stress on the special position of the poet occurs at the end of other centuries as well. Oscar Wilde, both in an 1885 review and in the 1890 essay "The Critic as Artist," designates the poet "the supreme artist."[20] Whether poetry, painting, or sculpture was the superior art was still at issue at the end of the nineteenth century. That artists, rather than monarchs, were the center of cultural authority was noncontroversial and hence not even addressed. (The "cultural life" of Dryden's assertion, notes Braudy, has been long.) At the turn from the nineteenth to the twentieth century, the question was not whether art was authoritative but only how "totalizing" that authority might become. If art could always, Yeats wrote in 1901, aspire to the intensity and dedication of current productions at Stratford-on-Avon, it would grow "serious as the Ten Commandments."[21]

It has been the argument here that poetry's persistent attention to "numbering"[22] may be one reason why it is so marked by the end of the century. Certainly the relation between numbered and unnumbered language—verse and prose—is itself a fin-de-siècle topic: Sidney addresses it (1595); Dryden addresses it (1697, 1700); Wordsworth addresses it (1800); Pater addresses it in his 1889 essay "Style," which also discusses Dryden's and Wordsworth's century-apart accounts.[23] The metrical experimentation that occurs at the ends of centuries reinforces attention to the subject: the first three books of The Faerie Queene appeared in 1590; the next three in 1596; Epithalamion in 1595. Spenser's metrical virtuosity and experimentation were already richly evident in the 1579 Shepheardes Calender;[24] and although that work greatly predates the fin de siècle, it surely validates the connection between metrical and calendric counting. A short 1899 treatise by William Johnson Stone called On the Use of Classical Meters in English assesses William Webbe's 1586 Discourse on English Poetry, George Puttenham's 1589 Art of English Poesie, and the influence of Abraham

Fraunce's experiments in hexameter on the poetry of Sidney and Spenser. Stone identifies the 1589 era as "the most fruitful period of metrical experiments." He argues that the metrical experimentation of the Elizabethans then disappeared for a long period and that its "revival" only took place with "Southey and his school"—that is, in the 1790s.[25] More recent theorists of meter, I. A. Richards and Paul Fussell, have speculated that it is because the beat in poetry takes place at a more accelerated rate than one's own heartbeat that it elicits a sense of excitement.[26] Perhaps the overtness with which calendric counting takes place at the end of the nineties (the century, according to Jorie Graham, "clicking by") causes this same press of rapidity and excitement. Wordsworth's long December 1799 letter—alternating all along between numbering and describing—suddenly surrenders at the very end to the exhilaration and exclamation of uninterrupted counting:

> We were in high spirits, and off we drove, and will you believe me when I tell you that we walked the next ten miles . . . thanks to the wind that drove behind us and the good road, in two hours and a quarter, a marvellous feat of which D. will long tell. Well! we rested . . . and then off to Sedbergh 7 miles farther in an hour and thirty five minutes, the wind was still at our backs. . . . I must hurry on, next morning we walked to Kendal, 11 miles, a terrible up and down road, in 3 hours, and after buying and ordering furniture, the next day by half past four we reached Grasmere in a post chaise. So ends my long story. God bless you. W. W.[27]

The acceleration incited by the mounting proximity of Grasmere seems redoubled by the rush to post the letter—"I must hurry on"— and place it in Coleridge's hands before the 7s turned to 8s.

A second reason why the turn of the century may impress itself on poetry is the peculiarly difficult relation between the human will and fin-de-siècle engagements with the calendar. Allen Grossman's 1990 *Summa Lyrica* (subtitled *A Primer of the Commonplaces in Speculative Poetics*) opens by identifying the central aspiration of poetry: "The function of poetry is to obtain for everybody a kind of success at the limits of the autonomy of the will. . . . Poetry serves to obtain a kind of outcome . . . precisely at those points where the natural will is helpless."[28] Many of the major descriptive terms associated with the fin de siècle—lassitude, malaise, enervation—suggest the way the calendar (although itself a humanly invented artifact) imperils the individual will. When, in contrast, one draws a picture of the human will based on the *poetic* legacy of final decades, a very different portrait emerges: the many poems already invoked here—poems, for example, by Chaucer, Sidney, Shakespeare, Spenser, Blake, Coleridge, Wordsworth—suggest that the end of the century inspires inaugurating linguistic acts, words, lines, passages, plays that invigorate the language not just of the next century but of a period far into the future. The end of the century, in other words, far from contracting one's belief in one's own agency, seems instead to prompt the desire to reconstitute the world linguistically. A related area of linguistic endowment which becomes especially marked in final decades is the contractual. Margreta de Grazia speaks of the way millenarianism sometimes inspires political reform, "most consequentially by Parliamentarians"; and Leo Braudy's essay is centrally devoted to the way in which the publication of Locke's *Two Treatises of Government* in the 1690s, coupled with a shift to parliamentary rather than monarchic power, inaugurates a world whose beneficiaries resided in (not the next but) the next three centuries. Thomas Paine's *Rights of Man* of the 1790s is, as Martin Green observes in *Prophets of a New Age,* the same kind of attempt to inaugurate a new world, to provide the tools by which a new world might successfully get built; and Green persuasively argues that the 1890s are also characterized by people who take on themselves responsibility for the next century, figures such as Gandhi, whose work in the nineties was dedicated to the parliamentary and constitutional.[29]

Final decades, then, at once disempower and reinvigorate the human will, a coupling that bears out Yeats' observation that "only the greatest obstacle that can be contemplated without despair rouses the will to full intensity."[30] The peculiar combination of enervation and revivification is observable even in a much smaller unit of time such as the transition to a new year: the end of the old year comes upon us like winter, something that we can (however vigorous or vague our preparation) do nothing to alter. Yet the widespread custom of "New Year's resolutions" demonstrates the way that ending simultaneously revivifies the will, incites the will to confidence. The century's end provides a far more enervating problem for at least four reasons: the radius of the will, the impossibility of sequence, the disappearance of adjacency, and the loss of self-description. (And it is these problems, rather than the mystery of how they are overcome by poets and political actors, which are briefly unfolded below.)

First, the scale of the period—one hundred years—places it outside the radius of the human will. Thomas Hardy, for example, was normally comfortable with endings. He inhabited them. As a child he each evening sat alone by a staircase wall that had been painted "Venetian red" to watch its hue intensify in the setting sun and recite ("with great fervency") the hymn "And now another day is gone."[31] As an adult, he recorded the precise sequence in which the trees in any given year dropped their leaves: "The order in which the leaves fall this year is: Chestnuts; Sycamores; Limes; Hornbeams, Elm; Birch; Beech."[32] Yet, unlike these other calendric units, the century's end could never be comfortable because the hundred-year unit was itself uninhabitable. He returns to its uninhabitability again and again, not only in his overt elegy for the nineteenth century, "Darkling Thrush"—dated December 31, 1900, and originally titled "By the Century's Deathbed"—but also in a set of poems that describe his house either one hundred years prior to or posterior to his own inhabiting of it. "Domicilium," the first poem he ever wrote, includes in its description of his childhood cottage at Bockhampton an oak from a seed "dropped by some bird a hundred years ago"; and the later poem, "The Strange House: Max Gate, A.D. 2000," describes, as its subtitle specifies, the house he lived in as an adult a century after his presence there. In 1867 he wrote a poem entitled "1967": "In five-score summers! All new eyes, / New minds, new modes, new fools, new wise." And throughout the late 1890s he returns often to the hundred-year unit, or its close approximation: the seventy-six-year-long orbit of Halley's comet ("The Comet at Yell'ham"); the 110th anniversary of the midnight on which Gibbon wrote the last sentence of *Decline and Fall* ("Lausanne: In Gibbon's Old Garden: 11–12 p.m.").[33]

The hundred-year period is anomalously called "a period" because, *experientially,* the one thing it can never be is periodic: like a comet, the fin de siècle may arc through one's lifetime once, but it is highly unlikely to do so two or three times. Therefore it asserts sequence while placing the sequential beyond us. Those who live inside the year

2000 may refer to it as the jubilee year, as Hillel Schwartz shows was true of 1300, 1500, 1600, 1700, and 1900,[34] but one will not use the word with any palpable sense of the accrued weight that comes with its return. On January 1, 2001, people may well exchange New Century greetings and New Century gifts, as they did on January 1, 1701, and again in 1801, and again in 1901;[35] but though we will know that it is an end-of-century practice, there will be no felt fact of it as a practice, no sense of the commitedness that accompanies the habitual and the rhythmic, the inhabitably arhythmetic. Like Ashbery's "The Plural of Jack-in-the-Box," it is even hard to determine exactly how to write the plural of fin de siècle.

Against this impossibility of experiential sequence is the poet's own act of lifting forward, making sensuously available, the phenomenon of sequence. "When one reads Blake," Yeats wrote in 1897, "it is as though the spray of an inexhaustible fountain of beauty was blown into our faces."[36] Yeats, in the *Autobiographies,* says that he and a friend entered the nineties by undertaking a four-year project of studying Blake's prophetic books: "We took it as almost a sign of Blake's personal help when we discovered that the spring of 1889, when we first joined our knowledge, was one hundred years from the publication of *The Book of Thel,* the first published of the 'Prophetic Books', as though it were firmly established that the dead delight in anniversaries."[37] Given this sensitivity to hundred-year periods, and to the decade of the nineties to which the *Autobiographies* are primarily devoted, it seems plausible that he thought of himself as writing about the 1390s, the 1590s, and the 1790s when, near the end of the first book, he summarizes the trajectory of English literature by imagining Chaucer's pilgrims climbing onto an Elizabethan stage, then reemerging once more in romantic poetry: "Chaucer's personages had disengaged themselves from Chaucer's crowd, forgot their common goal and shrine, and after sundry magnifications became each in turn the centre of some Elizabethan play, and had after split into their elements and so given birth to romantic poetry."[38]

This bridging back across ends of centuries appears in other writers as well. When Pater attends to Dryden's and Wordsworth's accounts of the relation between prose and verse, he consciously notes that Wordsworth is writing one hundred years after Dryden, and he is surely not unmindful of the fact that he in turn is writing one hundred years after Wordsworth. Again, Hardy in the year 1900, one hundred years after the "Preface" to the *Lyrical Ballads,* makes diary entries attempting to clarify Wordsworth's use of the word *imagination,* as well as charts displaying his own conception of the overlays and separations between the three terms Wordsworth sorted out: verse, the language of common speech, and poetic diction. Florence Emily Hardy records these diary entries shortly before her all-capitalized break in the biography, "END OF THE NINETEENTH CENTURY."[39]

This sequencing is important because with the experiential impossibility of sequence comes a third disempowering event, the falling away of the century that used to be adjacent to our own: the nineteenth century, the thing by which we knew ourselves if only because it steadily neighbored us with its differences, will suddenly be out of our reach, interrupted by this other overfull thing, this big thing in the way, the twentieth century, which will seem strangely intrusive in its adjacency, even when it is constituted by our own acts and objects, our wars and our poems. The beloved predecessor—with its Shelleys and Brontës and Austen and Eliot—will slip over the horizon, blocked from view by this other crammed-full thing, and be demoted to the nonprecursor status, the diffuse pastness, of the eighteenth century or the Renaissance.

With this comes a fourth disempowering event, the loss of the power of self-description. The time allotted to any population to give an account of themselves eventually runs out; soon it becomes other people's turn to describe them. Even the names by which we are called will probably not be of own choosing. The arithmetic is, in this regard, once more exceptional: it provides a reliable vehicle of self-representation, since it ensures some measure of continuity between what one calls oneself—"twentieth century"—and what one is called by later peoples. In contrast, the nonarithmetic names by which an era designates itself—modern and postmodern, for example—are unlikely to be the ones by which the period will be designated three centuries later. Even if people name themselves by a favorite invention of the period—age of air, jet age, atomic age, computer age, century of cinema, high tech—it is unlikely to stand; we usually now refer to the "age of steam" only when we are talking about steam-drawn trains and how the people of the period quaintly called themselves by that name.[40] Even the dynastic names—ones coming from the governor (Elizabethan) or from an attribute of the government (Augustan, Restoration)—tend to come long after the fact: the *Oxford English Dictionary*'s first recorded use for "Elizabethan" (1558–1603) is 1807;[41] for "Georgian" (1714–1820) is 1855; for "Restoration" (1660 and following) is 1728. Even if a period is self-named, as were the Victorians and again the twentieth-century Georgians, the cluster of connotations may change radically as soon as the self-namers are gone: the Victorians named themselves but had not in mind the dismissive connotations the word had acquired by 1918, when Pound would speak of "the odour of defunct Victoriana," or by 1934, when the word appeared in *Webster's* defined as "prudish, strict; old-fashioned, out-dated."[42] Perhaps (like people not only in Victorian Britain but in the "Victorian" United States and "Victorian" Germany) we will all in the twentieth century eventually be named for a British queen: we could be called the Second Elizabethans. Or perhaps like early-twentieth-century Georgian Green, we will come to be identified by what is eventually perceived as the century's characteristic color (Second Elizabethan Neon).

This elegy to the lost power of self-naming simply summarizes the more important and complicated surrender of the power of self-description. The last chance for self-description puts a special pressure on language and on the great wielders of language, as Barbara Smith's *Poetic Closure* and Frank Kermode's *Sense of an Ending* have made so enduringly visible. Even the ending of a solitary life incites this special attention to language. In his 1992 *Last Words,* Karl Guthke examines the many-centuries-long cultural preoccupation with the last sentence that people have spoken before dying, the thick tradition of both authentic and inauthentic narratives about the final words of Montaigne, Goethe, Socrates, and hundreds of others. The long history of anthologizing those final words began in the seventeenth century and then became more generalized and accelerated from the mid-nineteenth century forward.[43] It is even the case that the law in many countries—possibly all countries, writes Guthke—gives a special status to dying words. Hearsay, for example, is ordinarily inadmissible in Anglo-American law; but if the hearsay is spoken by a person immediately before death (naming the murderer, for example), an exception is made; the testimony is counted as legitimate evidence and is admissible in a court of law.[44] At issue here is the exit line of an individual person, not the exit lines of entire populations inhabiting a given century. But something of the same pressure toward acute self-description must surely be at work in the larger sphere, and this cultural desire to find appropriate "final" sentences partly explains the rapt attention to poets, to those whose powers of language are most rigorous. Even, then, in the midst of fin-de-siècle pluralism, the free-for-all of open voices, there is the sense of the circle drawing back, the clearing being made, to hear the voice of Seamus Heaney or Jorie Graham. And as the approaching "turn" increases the longing for language, so language (continually recontextualized into the ever greater lateness of the nineties) itself undergoes a magnification, a "latening." In 1896, the question was whether *Jude the Obscure* was the best or worst book of the year.[45] By 1899, the question was whether it was the best or worst book of the century.[46]

The four forms of disempowering the will—the radius of one hundred years, the impossibility of experiencing sequence, the disappearance of the predecessor, the loss of the power of self-description—all entail the past and present. An even greater problem is the future. What the twentieth century will have been can still be greatly changed by what now occurs in the final few years; but most of its canvas is filled. The future century, in contrast, is vast and open. The knownness of the past and unknownness of the future is, of course, a source of disablement not just in final decades but in all decades: Allen Grossman speaks of the ongoing "asymmetry of consciousness," its inclusion of what is over, its noninclusion of what has not yet happened.[47] But the turning of a century draws attention to and heightens (latens) the discomfort of that asymmetry. "Here we are in a new reign, & with a general sense of the unknown lying round us," writes Hardy in February 1901.[48] Here we are, he might have written, borrowing Jorie Graham's 1991 title, in the "Region of Unlikeness."

So WE RETURN to the calendric nature of poetry and the poet's desire "to obtain a kind of outcome . . . precisely at those points where the natural will is helpless," to enter the calendar, to alter it, to make it an active verb ("I . . . shall calendar an evening spent with you on so

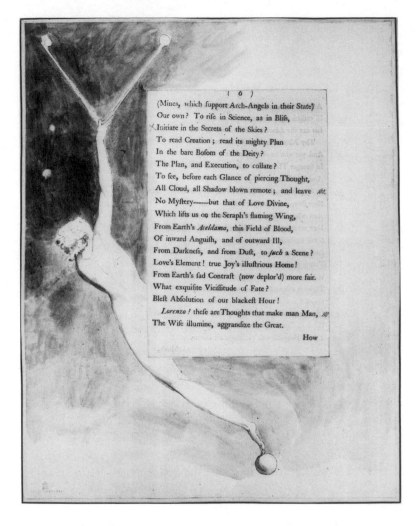

William Blake. Watercolor illustration for Edward Young's Night Thoughts.
Night Six, lines 93–111. 1796. British Museum, London.

interesting a subject among my noctes atticae," writes Coleridge to Godwin in the January 1800 letter about 7s and 8s), to place the century within the radius of the human will.

Like the *Canterbury Tales,* Chaucer's *Treatise on the Astrolabe* was written in the final decade of the 1300s. It is, in fact, the only work by Chaucer which is explicitly dated in its own interior:[49] March 12, 1391, recurs several times. It is addressed to the ten-year-old child Lewis who would come of age in the next century when Chaucer, who died in 1400, would no longer be present. The treatise moves lovingly over the concrete surface of the astrolabe—"forget not thys, litel Lowys"[50]—requiring the child to commit its intricately detailed surface to memory. It places within his grasp, confers as legacy, the ability to locate horizon and zenith, the twenty-four hours of the day, the rise and fall of the stars, the movements of the moon. Bright, beautiful toy, it enables its user not simply to distinguish and demarcate day and night but to find the precise moment when night becomes dawn, or when evening gives way to night; "to knowe the spryng of the dawneyng" and to "fynd in the bordure the ende of the evenyng, that is verrey nyght."[51] Like Donne's compasses of the 1590s or Blake's compasses of the 1790s, Chaucer's astrolabe is a material locus of empowerment: it places the person in an active or volitional relation to the calendar.

Perhaps poetry written in the final decade of a century should be seen under the rubric (borrowed from Wordsworth) of the "evening voluntary," for much of it is devoted to finding the precise moment when one thing ends and another begins: to "fynd in the bordure the ende of the evenyng, that is verrey nyght." The poems that Wordsworth entitled "Evening Voluntaries" were written in the 1830s. But their care to calibrate the passage of growing night—

> Look for the stars, you'll say that there are none;
> Look up a second time, and, one by one,
> You mark them twinkling out . . .
>
> (I, lines 3–5)

—recurs again and again throughout the poetry of the 1790s such as *Descriptive Sketches,* which presents the same scene at "Sunset," "Twilight," and "Morning," and *An Evening Walk,* whose opening argument maps the poem's passage across "Sunset," "Twilight Objects," "Twilight Sounds," "Western Lights," "Night," "Moonlight," and "Night Sounds." It is descriptive of the work of many others as well: William Blake's 1796 watercolor drawings of Young's *Night Thoughts* (he made more than five hundred of them); Thomas Hardy's turn-of-the-century poems about crossing the transition line of midnight; Frank Bidart's two long poems of 1991, "In the First Hour of the Night" (a poem that initiates the act of counting, for it is the start of a series of long poems about the successive hours of the night) and "In the Western Night," a poem whose title, says Seamus Heaney, "can evoke the balm and romance of the Pacific Coast of California and at the same time intimate the burnt-out categories of European civilization in the late twentieth century."[52] In its musical context, the voluntary (a term first used in 1597) is a devotional composition usually marking the terminal points, the beginning or end, of a religious service: it is "voluntary" in that its inclusion is at the discretion of the organist, who is wholly at liberty to originate the piece, which is at once "inspirational" and "improvisational."[53]

It is not just the calendar whose interior is entered and altered (the calendar is, after all, from its outset a human construct) but the natural events in behind it: stars, sky, blossoms are themselves hybridized with human artfulness. The garden—call it the garden voluntary—is to the calendar year what the evening voluntary is to the calendar day. The attempt to recuperate the human will is most overt in those centuries in which garden and calendar are allied with the monarch, either in portraits of the ruler given by poets or in the ruler's own self-portrait. Elizabeth, for example, was perceived as the eglantine rose, and the poetic hybridization of queen with flower extends, as Roy Strong writes in *The Renaissance Garden in England,* from the April eclogue in Spenser's 1579 *Shepheardes Calender* to John Davies' twenty-six *Hymnes to Astraea* of 1600, in which the letters of her name, ELIZABETH REGINA, provide the starting places for a crossweave of calendar and flowers: *E* generates the line "*Empresse of flowers . . .*"; *T* becomes "*The new fresh* Houres *and Graces*"; *R* starts the line "*Roses and lillies did them draw.*"[54] For William III in the 1690s, the garden served as a form of self-portrait: in that decade, he lavished eighty-eight thousand pounds on his gardens, a figure estimated to be half of all expenses on his

William Rogers. Engraving. Elizabeth I as 'Rosa
Electa' flanked by Tudor Roses and Eglantine.
c. 1590–1600. British Museum, London.

palaces.[55] Appropriately, he was perceived by contemporaries (if not as
rose or lily, still) as a gardener—as much "a *Gard'ner* as he was a *Sol-
dier.*"[56] Queen Mary, who originated the post of "Queen's Botanist,"[57]
shared William's devotion; and together they inspired in the British
population the fever of personal gardens which Leo Braudy describes[58]
and which is also described in Peter Greenaway's film about the 1690s,
The Draughtsman's Contract.[59] Even, then, by the 1690s the garden is
distributed to a widening population: by the 1790s and the 1890s it is
not the monarch's garden but the cottage garden that is central.[60]

The fin-de-siècle entry of the artist into the realm of blossoms has

Eugène Grasset. La Belle Jardinière, *"July." 1896.*
Museum for Arts and Crafts, Hamburg.

its most visually familiar registration in the omnipresent, stylized plants of art nouveau, many of whose practitioners were deeply influenced by the Swiss-French artist Eugene Grasset, whose range of flower designs is compressed in *La plante et ses applications ornamentales* (1896).[61] Grasset's practice, amidst that of William Morris and many other British and Continental designers, is of particular interest because his work makes visible the inseparability of garden and calendar. The twelve prints of the 1896 *La Belle Jardinière,* for example, were originally commissioned as a calendar for the Parisian department store Bon Marché. Shoulder deep in huge red poppies and white lilies (their cups supporting her as though she were only another flower in their midst), the beautiful gardener of July repeats in the folds and form of her dress and scarf the breezy shapes of the blossoms. As though to merge garden voluntary with evening voluntary, the tissue of her dress (as is true in the other eleven months as well) is imprinted with an abstract skywriting of celestial signs. Grasset had ten years earlier done a calendar for Bon Marché based exclusively on plants and zodiac signs.[62] His plant-filled cover illustrations during the 1890s for magazines such as *L'illustration* and *Harpers*[63] were themselves calendric, since such magazines came in weekly or monthly installments. Plants, flowers, and gardens appeared throughout the visual and verbal arts of the nineties (Yeats' *The Rose* was published in 1893, *The Wind among the Reeds* in 1899) in Britain and other countries. It is not accidental, for example, that almost a third of Carl Schorske's classic study *Fin-de-siècle Vienna* is devoted to chapters with titles such as "The Transformation of the Garden" and "Explosion in the Garden."[64]

But the devotion to blossoms, at least in England, typifies other final decades as well. Wordsworth's Grasmere letter of late December 1799—its curtain of water falling over rocks colored dove, violet, yellow, purple, black and "covered with water-plants of the most vivid green"—is suggestive of the place of gardens at the century's turn, as well as backward through the preceding decade. Among the illuminated plates of Blake's *Book of Thel* and *Songs of Innocence and Experience,* there is barely a page where the poem is not companioned by the arching illustration of a tree, plant, flower that seems to wish to enclose, shelter (or at least co-inhabit the space of) the linguistic events. Often—as in the pages for "Infant Joy" and "The Blossom"—the dramatic personae themselves reside along the inner surface of the delicate blossom; and always, always, the letters of the poems break into the "leafy flourishes," "tendrils," and "trailing vines" that commentators have described with such precision: "The italic capitals of '*BOOK*' " begins David Erdman's commentary on the *Book of Thel,* "are alive with sinuous leaves that make buds of the three plump letters and form, against the '*K*,' a calyx from which curved stamens rise in a pattern repeated in the soaring forms rising from blossoms of a similar shape at page bottom."[65] Back in behind Blake one can sense the presence of what Jerome McGann calls the "vocal landscapes" and "the luscious pages" of the Della Cruscans.

This desire to yoke acts of linguistic origination or verbal creation

William Blake. Song of Los. *Plate 5, copy D. 1795.*
British Museum, London.

with vegetation occurs in the 1690s, the 1590s, and forward into the 1990s as well. Dryden's belief announced in 1694, that poetry originated with the Garden, was no doubt influenced by the fact that he himself had spent the year translating Vergil's *Pastorals* and *Georgics*.[66] Throughout the 1590s appear the "honeysuckle villains" of Shakespeare's histories and the "luscious woodbine" of the comedies. The fictive persons often come to seem hybrids of verse and flowers, not only in the most flower filled of all the plays, *A Midsummer Night's Dream* (1594–95), in which three of the characters are blossoms, but even in the tragedies at the century's turn and a few years afterward.[67] Ophelia, as her brother sees, is continuous with the columbine and meadow rue, the blue-veined pansies and violets that might seem only her "fantastic garlands,"[68] just as Lear is continuous with the nettles and cuckoo flowers of his wildflower crown. To inhabit the creative word is, for Shakespeare almost as much as for Blake, to inhabit a blossom: "Where the bee sucks, there suck I / In a cowslip's bell I lie," says Ariel on behalf of a poet for whom the whole of England is a "sea-walled garden" and islands are apples that can be closed in a hand or a pocket seeding other islands the following year.[69]

The evening voluntary and the garden voluntary, though never confined to the ends of centuries, continually recur there. It is as though in ordinary times we are content to permit the construct of the calendar to exist in a loose analogic relation to the events of sky and ground which lie behind it (barely remembering that Sunday is Sunday, Monday is Moon-day, that spring began as "spring of the leaf"), or as though the calendar were a huge semitransparent curtain very loosely draped in front of, and hence often swinging away from, those celestial and material events. And it is as though the turning of the century, in contrast, could only be accomplished by somehow, for a time, bringing the calendar into more precise alignment with those anterior events, pulling the curtain back (like Wordsworth's waterfall), or making it fully transparent, or pinning its contours to the thick shapes and sounds that lie, now newly exposed, behind. Or perhaps the calendar isn't draped over the events at all but can, by cutting those events open, be found inside: like Seamus Heaney cutting open roots, "And, at the centre, a dark watermark. / O calendar customs!"[70] Seamus Heaney—for whom the felt experience of the poem's coming into being is like a plant and the poem's effect is like the wet cutting blades of holly and ice[71]—repeatedly locates poetic consciousness at ground level. As a child, he first recognized that he was to be a poet on a day when, covered with nets and twigs, he mimed a thicket and spoke as a "shaking bush";[72] and his poems repeatedly place him underground,[73] or prone on the ground (looking up at the sky through a mat of sweetpea), or even when standing on the ground, submerged and surrounded ("waist-deep in cow-parsley").[74] This sense of poetic making as occurring in the space from which plants grow is reaffirmed in the way he pictures the formation of other poets. His account of poetic making in Hardy centers on the child's head thrown back onto a grassy space, and his account of poetic making in Wordsworth centers on a picture (drawn from Dorothy's 1802 diary) of Dorothy and William lying prone on the ground, heads back, faces skyward: "Phrases like 'diurnal course' and 'diurnal roll' are underwritten by sensation and take their lifeline from moments like this."[75] The calendar is verified.

At evening, in the garden, the century ends but the world stays fresh. In its connotations of coolness, moisture, and sweetness, that which is fresh primarily addresses the senses of touch and taste. It derives from the old Germanic *frisk,* "fresh of temperature, hence unfaded, unwithered, also recent,"[76] and describes that which is "newly made, cool."[77] It is connected to the Italian word *fresco,* "to paint upon a fresh, still moist plaster."[78] Its early meaning as "unsalted" or "sweet"[79] generates a set of connotations that include "pure, sweet, eager"[80] or "eager and ardent,"[81] bringing to mind Seamus Heaney's observation that "blooming" means "impatient" as well as "flourishing."[82] At the ends of centuries "the fresh" ceases to be exclusively adjectival and begins to occupy all grammatical positions. It first appears as a noun in 1596 when the word *freshet* ("fresh water flowing into the sea") is formed, and 1596 is also the year when the noun *freshman* is first recorded. Its first appearance as the verb *to freshen* occurs in 1697.[83]

The sense that the ends of centuries have been bound up with poems, constitutions, and gardens is perhaps as much a performative as a descriptive: here, in the 1990s, in our own final decade, "let it be the case that there will be . . ." or "I wish that there might be . . ." poems, constitutions, and gardens. Writing to the author of *Political Justice* in September 1800, Coleridge sent kisses to Godwin's two little girls, then expressed the "wish" that they might all three move to a house near his own, then (seeing the unlikelihood of this outcome) observed that the linguistic construction "I wish" is "privileged" to have almost anything following it.[84] The end of the century is a period in which the performative and the descriptive often become for a time indistinguishable.

Poetry, says Allen Grossman, is not just the wish we make but the promise we make "against our vanishing."[85] In Blake's *Book of Thel* (1789), the young girl Thel (whose name is the Greek word for "wish" or "will")[86] speaks first to a Lily and then to a Little Cloud. The cloud asks, "Fearest thou because I vanish and am seen no more / Nothing remains?"[87] This conversation between girl and sky continues in Yeats' *A Vision* (1934): "My imagination goes some years backward," he writes, "and I remember a beautiful young girl singing at the edge of the sea in Normandy words and music of her own composition. . . . [She] sang with lifted head of the civilizations that there had come and gone, ending every verse with the cry: 'O lord, let something remain.' "[88] Thel and the beautiful Normandy singer are in turn joined by other singers on other waterways (the river Avon, the coast of Galway); for Yeats, in his turn-of-the-century essay on Stratford-on-Avon, describes the vivacity of the "strange procession of kings and queens" he has just seen in a group of plays (all written between 1590 and 1599),[89] *King John, Richard II, Second Part of Henry IV, Henry V, Second Part of Henry VI,* and *Richard III.* Watching them, he says, "I have felt as I have sometimes felt on grey days on the Galway shore, when a faint mist has hung over the grey sea and the grey stones, as if the world might suddenly vanish and leave nothing behind, not even a little dust under one's feet."[90] And in his essay on Edmund Spenser written a year later (1902), he discovers that his constant dread that a company of people will "then suddenly vanish" has it origins in another end-of-century work, the vision of Scudamour in *The Faerie Queene.*[91] The edge of the calendar itself becomes a shoreline on which a company of people gathers—Thel, the beautiful Normandy singer, Spenser, Shakespeare, and Yeats—making the shared promise "against our vanishing."

The precise character of the company and the changing shape of the promise are made visible in the essays that follow.

NOTES

1. Thomas Hardy, "To Sir George Douglas, Dec. 30, 1899, Max Gate, Dorchester," in *Collected Letters of Thomas Hardy,* vol. 2, *1893–1901,* ed. R. L. Purdy and M. Millgate (Oxford: Clarendon, 1980), 243. Because of the numerical drama of the change from 99 to 100, writers' responses to the new century are as likely to show up here as in the official turning over of the century in the transition from 00 to 01; hence both temporal locations are drawn upon throughout this introduction.

2. William Wordsworth, "Preface to the Second Edition of Several of the Foregoing Poems Published, with an Additional Volume, Under the Title of 'Lyrical Ballads,' " in *Wordsworth: Poetical Works (with Introductions and Notes),* 2d ed., ed. Thomas Hutchinson, rev. Ernest de Selincourt (New York: Oxford University Press, 1936), 734, 735. All subsequent references to the poetry and prefaces of Wordsworth are to this edition.

3. Wordsworth (paraphrasing Coleridge), "Essay, Supplementary to the Preface," 750.

4. Seymour Papert, "The Mathematical Unconscious," in *On Aesthetics in Science,* ed. Judith Wechsler (Cambridge: MIT Press, 1978), p. 111–13.

5. Hillel Schwartz calls attention to Dante's temporal setting in *Century's End: A Cultural History of the Fin de Siècle from the 990s through the 1990s* (New York: Doubleday, 1990), 63. Although Schwartz's wonderfully detailed century-by-century account begins with the 990s, he designates the 1290s (and hence the jubilee year 1300) as the first "publicly celebrated" end of century and attributes the timing in part to the fact that people had, for the first time, an "arithmetic sense of the passage of time" (55). Different cultural historians assign different starting dates to the fin de siècle: Margreta de Grazia in this volume, for example, directs us to as late a date as the 1790s.

6. A. Kent Hieatt, *Short Time's Endless Monument: The Symbolism of the Numbers in Edmund Spenser's 'Epithalamion'* (New York: Columbia University Press, 1960), 9–15. See also Hieatt, "The Daughters of Horus: Order in the Stanzas of *Epithalamion,*" in *Form and Convention in the Poetry of Edmund Spenser,* ed. William Nelson (New York: Columbia University Press, 1961), 103–21.

7. Walter Pater, "Aesthetic Poetry" (first published in *Westminster Review* [1868], first collected in *Appreciations* [1889]), in *Walter Pater: Essays on Literature and Art,* ed. and intro. Jennifer Uglow (London: Everyman's, 1973), 111. The subgenre of the nocturne which Pater locates in *Romeo and Juliet* is the aubade, but the aubade conflated with two other forms of love lyric, the sonnet and the epithalamion.

8. Thomas Hardy, "To Nathaniel Sparks, January 18, 1901, Dorchester,"

in *Collected Letters of Thomas Hardy,*" 2:278. This is Hardy's first letter of 1901, a thank-you note to Sparks for the "New Century gift" he had sent.

9. Samuel Taylor Coleridge, "To William Godwin, January 8, 1800," in *Collected Letters of Samuel Taylor Coleridge,* vol. 1, *1785–1800,* ed. Earl Leslie Griggs (Oxford: Clarendon, 1956), 560. I am grateful to Hillel Schwartz for directing my attention to this letter.

10. William Wordsworth, "W. W. and D. W. to S. T. Coleridge, Christmas Eve [and Dec. 27], Grasmere [1799]," in *The Letters of William and Dorothy Wordsworth: The Early Years, 1787–1805,* ed. Ernest de Selincourt, rev. Chester L. Shaver (Oxford: Clarendon, 1967), 273–82. Although only one sentence at the end is directly written by Dorothy Wordsworth, the entire letter is saturated with her presence. For a draft of the letter, see Appendix 5 in the volume.

11. Their first garden is described by Dorothy Wordsworth in "D. W. to Mrs. John Marshall, September 10th [and 12, 1800,] [Grasmere]," in *The Letters of William and Dorothy Wordsworth,* 293–301. Although the roses and honeysuckle have only the first year's growth, she says, the garden is "covered all over with the green leaves and scarlet flowers" that they have "trained . . . upon threads."

12. William Wordsworth, "W. W. and D. W. to S. T. Coleridge, Christmas Eve [and Dec. 27], Grasmere [1799]," 280. As it turned out, July of 1800 was devoted to preparing the second edition of the *Lyrical Ballads.* In order to carry this out, Coleridge joined William and Dorothy Wordsworth in Grasmere from June 29 to July 23. Among the changes made at that time was one that arranged for the addition of lines—"he was like a plant / Fair to the sun, the darling of the winds"—to Wordsworth's poem "Lines Left upon a Seat in a Yew-tree" ("S. T. C. and D. W. and W. W. to Messrs. Biggs and Cottle [Grasmere, mid-July 1800]," in *The Letters of William and Dorothy Wordsworth,* 185, 186).

13. *William Godwin: His Friends and Contemporaries* [Letters, Memoirs, and Editor's Commentary], ed. C. Kegan Paul (Boston, 1876), 1:354.

14. Austin Clarke, *The Celtic Twilight and the Nineties,* intro. Roger McHugh (Dublin: Dolmen Press, 1970), 50, 51.

15. Larry D. Benson, "The Canon and Chronology of Chaucer's Works," in *The Riverside Chaucer,* 3d ed., ed. F. N. Robinson (New York: Houghton Mifflin, 1987), xxix. Benson dates the General Prologue between 1388 and 1392.

Derek Pearsall (*The Life of Geoffrey Chaucer* [Oxford: Blackwell, 1992], 215, 226–30) sees work on the General Prologue possibly beginning as early as 1387. The framing dates for the whole of the *Canterbury Tales* are securely set at 1387 to 1400, though the precise dating for individual tales within that period is, as Pearsall argues, extremely "fragile." He observes, for example, the lack of actual evidence for the widespread identification of the Parson's Tale as a late tale.

My argument here is only the fact that the end of the century seems to draw forth acts of poetic genius, such as the *Canterbury Tales,* and not that such works are themselves *about* the end of the century. That second argument, however, can of course be made. For an assessment of the eschatological in the *Canterbury Tales,* see the bibliography given by Penn Szittya in "Domesday Bokes," in *The Apocalypse in the Middle Ages,* ed. Richard K. Emmerson and Bernard McGinn (Ithaca, N.Y.: Cornell University Press, 1992), 384.

16. Albert S. Cook argues that it was probably written around 1583 and that it was in circulation by 1589, since it begins to be cited in works by George Puttenham in 1589 and Sir John Harington in 1591 (introduction to *The Defence of Poesy, Otherwise Known as an Apology for Poetry,* by Sir Philip Sidney, ed. and intro. Albert S. Cook [New York, 1890], xii, xxxix).

17. John Dryden, "To Sir Godfrey Kneller," lines 89–92, in James Anderson Winn, *John Dryden and His World* (New Haven: Yale University Press, 1987), 470.

18. John Dryden, *Dedication of the Aeneid,* in Winn, *John Dryden and His World,* 486.

19. We are used to the fact that certain dynastic names—Elizabethan, Victorian—are often used to refer to the writers of the period. One might wrongly assume that this designation is only one among scores of possibilities, that just as for literary critics "Elizabethans" refers to the writers of the period, so for an astronomer the word would designate the astronomers, or for a merchant, the merchants. But according to the *Oxford English Dictionary* (hereafter *OED*), most of these period terms do have as their primary meaning—listed directly after the historical designation of the period by the monarch—the group of writers living during the period. (Occasionally, the word's primary meaning goes to some other art, the way "Georgian" refers most centrally to architecture.) This odd feature of the calendar underscores the shift of cultural centrality from the monarch to the writer. In other words, while the major democratic shift is registered in the way the arithmetic calendar comes to dominate over the dynastic one, even the dynastic one is retrospectively modified to refer almost as much to the period's artists as to its governors.

20. Richard Ellmann, *Oscar Wilde* (New York: Vintage, 1988), 312. For Wilde's and Pater's preference for prose over verse, see p. 84.

21. William Butler Yeats, "At Stratford-on-Avon" (1901), in *Essays and Introductions* (London: Macmillan, 1961), 99. For an account of the totalizing impulse at the first exhibition of the Secessionist movement in Vienna (1898),

see James Shedel, *Art and Society: The New Art Movement in Vienna, 1897–1914* (Palo Alto: Society for the Promotion of Science, 1981), 37, 38, 40, 41.

22. Paul Fussell points out that, especially in syllabic contexts, poets and readers often use the words *numbers* and *versification* as synonyms (*Poetic Meter and Poetic Form* [New York: Random House, 1965], 7).

23. Walter Pater, "Style," in *Walter Pater: Essays on Literature and Art*, 70, 71.

24. Especially the April, June, and August eclogues. See the introductory essays to the three in *The Yale Edition of the Shorter Poems of Edmund Spenser*, ed. William A. Oram, Einar Bjorvand, Ronald Bond, Thomas H. Cain, Alexander Dunlop, and Richard Schell (New Haven: Yale University Press, 1989), 67–69, 107–8, 135–36.

25. William Johnson Stone, *On the Use of Classical Metres in English* (London, 1899), 13, 16, 17. Paul Fussell mentions Stone's work, and its influence on later poets, in *Poetic Meter and Poetic Form*, 13.

26. Paul Fussell, Jr., *Poetic Meter and Poetic Form*, 5, 201, citing I. A. Richards' account of the physiological and psychological effects of meter in chapter 17 of *Principles of Literary Criticism* (New York: Harcourt, Brace, 1928).

27. William Wordsworth, "W. W. and D. W. to S. T. Coleridge, Christmas Eve [and Dec. 27], Grasmere [1799]," 280. Earlier in the letter, Wordsworth is explicit about the excitement caused by moving against a deadline: "We had a task of twenty one miles to perform in a short winter's day, all this put our minds in such a state of excitation that we were no unworthy spectators of this delightful scene" (278).

28. Allen Grossman, *Summa Lyrica: A Primer of the Commonplaces in Speculative Poetics, Western Humanities Review* 44, no. 1 (Spring 1990), 5, republished in *The Sighted Singer: Two Works on Poetry for Readers and Writers*, by Allen Grossman with Mark Halliday (Baltimore: Johns Hopkins University Press, 1992), 209.

29. Martin Green, *Prophets of a New Age: The Politics of Hope from the Eighteenth through the Twenty-first Centuries* (New York: Charles Scribner's Sons, 1992), 60–87, 118–44. I am grateful to Green for pointing out the way in which Gandhi's work in the 1890s emphasizes the constitutional (for example, Gandhi goes to London for a law degree, founds the Natal Indian Congress, initiates its members into the practice of debate, and so forth), even though Green himself actually argues that the parliamentarian and constitutional are too Western and nonradical to represent the "new age" mentality that Gandhi himself will display a few years later. Many other details in this book also bring in, somewhat incidentally, the constitutional.

The stress on the contractual at the ends of centuries is seen by some scholars as occurring earlier than the 1690s. On the connection, for example, between the beginning of the "rule of written law" and the *Domesday Book* (1086–88), see Szittya, "Domesday Bokes," 377.

30. W. B. Yeats, *The Trembling of the Veil,* "Book I: Four Years: 1887–1891," in *Autobiographies* (London: Macmillan, 1955), 195.

31. Florence Emily Hardy, *The Early Life of Thomas Hardy, 1840–1891: Compiled Largely from Contemporary Notes, Letters, Diaries, and Biographical Memoranda, as well as from Oral Information in Conversations Extending over Many Years* (New York: Macmillan, 1928), 19. According to Florence Emily Hardy, he would come to the wall before the "chromatic effect" had begun, in order to be in place "wait[ing]" for it to start.

32. Thomas Hardy, diary notes for "First Week in November [1905]," in Florence Emily Hardy, *The Later Years of Thomas Hardy, 1892–1928* (New York: Macmillan, 1930), 114.

33. Poets bring the seemingly unnegotiable hundred-year unit within the radius of the will by contracting the time (to a day or a year) or by magnifying it, as when Yeats begins to think in thousand-year cycles. The same is true of political actors. Throughout *The Rights of Man,* Thomas Paine examines the difference between inappropriately binding the future through monarchic inheritance (as well as contracts that preempt the decision making of future actors) and a legacy of rights that will be perpetually enabling: "A thousand years hence, those who shall live in America, or in France, will look back with contemplative pride on the origin of their governments, and say, *this was the work of our glorious ancestors!* But what can a monarchical talker say? . . . A certain something forbids him to look back to a beginning, lest some robber, or some Robin Hood, should rise from the obscurity of time and say, *I am the origin"* (*The Rights of Man, Part I,* in *Thomas Paine: Political Writings,* ed. Bruce Kuklick [Cambridge: Cambridge University Press, 1989], 120).

34. Schwartz, *Century's End,* 56–63, 94, 111, 192.

35. See Hardy's January 1901 letter mentioned in note 8 above; other instances of the "New Century" greeting occur passim in Schwartz.

36. W. B. Yeats, "William Blake and the Imagination" (1897), in *Essays and Introductions,* 113.

37. Yeats, *Trembling of the Veil,* "Book I," 161.

38. Ibid., 193. Yeats goes on to ask whether it is the work of his contemporaries to move the process of ever magnified subjectivity yet one stage further (as in his own case) or instead to begin to run the film backward (as in Tolstoy's case).

39. Florence Emily Hardy, *Later Years of Thomas Hardy,* 85, 87. Poets at the end of the twentieth century also acknowledge their continuity with earlier ends. As though in anticipation of her own fin-de-siècle lyrics, Jorie Graham in

1983 writes a poem explicitly about the 1890s, "Two Paintings by Gustav Klimt."

40. *OED,* 2d ed., s.v. "steam."

41. Though the citations for "Elizabethan" begin in 1807 and proceed throughout the nineteenth century, the *OED* does quote Masson's 1859 biography of Milton as saying: "The . . . literature of England would be represented to Milton, in the year 1624, by that cluster of . . . men . . . who had been already named 'the Elizabethans' " (*OED,* 2d ed., s.v. "Elizabethan"). Dates given for other dynastic names in this paragraph are also drawn from the *OED.*

42. *OED,* 2d ed., s.v. "Victorian."

43. See chapter 4, "Guidance, Entertainment, and Frisson: Anthologies of Last Words," in Karl S. Guthke, *Last Words: Variations on a Theme in Cultural History* (Princeton: Princeton University Press, 1992), 98–155.

44. Guthke, *Last Words,* 28. Guthke points out (37) that legal treatises on dying declarations from the late eighteenth century to the present always quote the dying words of Count Melun in Shakespeare's *King John* (c. 1596).

45. Thomas Hardy, "To William Archer, January 2, 1896, Max Gate, Dorchester," in *Collected Letters of Thomas Hardy,* 2:104, n.

46. Thomas Hardy, "To Florence Henniker, April 13, 1899, Max Gate, Dorchester," in *Collected Letters of Thomas Hardy,* 2:219. By this point the word *century* is so often invoked by Hardy that he often contracts it to *centy.*

47. Grossman, *Summa Lyrica,* 12.

48. "To Florence Henniker, February 15, 1901," in *Collected Letters of Thomas Hardy,* 2:280. The asymmetry between the almost completed century and the not-yet-started next century is powerfully expressed in Wordsworth's 1799 Grasmere letter in his emphasis on the brevity of the daylight in 1799 and the length of the daylight in 1800 (see note 27 above). Fin-de-siècle poets sometimes redress that asymmetry: Yeats opens his 1897 essay on Blake, "There have been men who loved the future like a mistress, and the future mixed her breath into their breath and shook her hair about them, and hid them from the understanding of their times. William Blake was one of these men, and if he spoke confusedly and obscurely it was because he spoke of things for whose speaking he could find no models in the world he knew" ("William Blake and the Imagination," 111).

49. Benson, "Canon and Chronology of Chaucer's Works," xxix. For a fascinating discussion of other calendars written during the 1380s and 1390s, and in particular the "shadow-tables" designed to enable one to determine the exact time of day from the length of one's own shadow, see Pearsall's *Life of Geoffrey Chaucer,* 217–20. Both the introduction to the Man of Law's Tale and

the Parson's Prologue allude to such shadow-tables (217). The Man of Law's Tale includes a passage on the equinoxes, and the temple visits in the Knight's Tale are compatible with the "calculations" on "planetary hours" in the *Treatise on the Astrolabe*. Pearsall also assesses the likelihood that Chaucer is the author of the 1392 *Equatorie of the Planetis* and that it is the promised continuation of the *Treatise on the Astrolabe* (219).

Pearsall observes, even in his chapter titles, the sense of "New Beginnings" from the late eighties onward and "Renewal" of the 1390s. What Pearsall calls Chaucer's "characteristic aversion to closure" (233) is perhaps also relevant to discussions of the calendar.

50. Geoffrey Chaucer, *Treatise on the Astrolabe,* part 1, in *The Works of Geoffrey Chaucer,* 2d ed., ed. F. N. Robinson (Boston: Houghton Mifflin, 1957), 547.

51. Ibid., 552.

52. Seamus Heaney, "Frank Bidart: A Salute," *Agni* 36 (1993), 270, 271 (Seamus Heaney's introduction to Frank Bidart's March 1992 Morris Gray Reading at Harvard University).

53. This description of the voluntary in music draws on the much more elaborate accounts provided in *OED*, 2d ed., s.v. "voluntary"; *New Oxford Companion to Music,* ed. Denis Arnold (New York: Oxford University Press, 1983), 2: 1947–48; and *Grove's Dictionary of Music and Musicians,* 5th ed., ed. Eric Blom (London: Macmillan, 1954), 9:71–72.

54. Roy Strong, *The Renaissance Garden in England* (London: Thames and Hudson, 1979), 44–48. Gardens, writes Strong, "remained an essential feature of the age, so potent that four centuries later we still think of the old formal gardens of England as being Elizabethan in style. We imagine that we know much more about Elizabethan gardens than in fact we do" (45).

55. John Harris, "The Architecture of the Williamite Court," in *The Age of William III and Mary II: Power, Politics, and Patronage, 1688–1702,* ed. Robert P. Maccubbin and Martha Hamilton-Phillips (Williamsburg, Va.: College of William and Mary, 1989), 229. I am grateful to Leo Braudy for bringing this extraordinary book to my attention.

56. Stephen Switzer (1715) cited by John Dixon Hunt, "A Lion in the Garden: The Anglo-Dutch Garden," in Maccubbin and Hamilton-Phillips, *William III and Mary II,* 238. For Defoe on King William, see William Thomas Stearn's essay "Horticulture and Botany," in the same volume, 181.

57. Stearn, "Horticulture and Botany," 185.

58. The fever of new gardens, nurseries, and greenhouses is in turn credited with having sponsored the conditions that led to the first hybrid in England, a cross between a carnation and a sweet william (Stearn, "Horticulture and

Botany," 183), though the event itself did not actually occur until 1717 (*Oxford Companion to Gardens,* ed. Goeffrey and Susan Jellicoe [Oxford: Oxford University Press, 1991], 267). Such hybridization, according to Stearn, was at first greeted with fear but soon gained momentum and by the nineteenth century was practiced without restraint. New hybrids appeared throughout the century; the first breakthrough hybridization of an orange rose—Austrian brier, *Rosa foetida*—occurred in 1891 (*Oxford Companion to Gardens,* 482).

59. Peter Greenaway's ingenious attention to the ends of centuries is visible not only in *The Draughtsman's Contract,* but also in *ZOO* (where any numeral might be inserted into the place of the "Z") and in *Drowning by Numbers,* where the narrative is paced across the act of counting to 100.

60. At the end of the nineteenth century and the turn into the twentieth, for example, William Robinson and Gertrude Jekyll greatly vivified and extended attention to the cottage garden through their garden landscape, published books, and weekly magazines. From 1892 to 1898, Robinson's weekly magazine *Cottage Gardening* (less expensive than the periodicals he had started as early as the seventies) distributed the vision to a much wider, more economically diverse population (Tom Turner, *English Garden Design: History and Styles since 1650* [Woodbridge, Suffolk: Antique Collectors' Club, 1986], 192–95; *Oxford Companion to Gardens,* s.v. "Cottage Garden," "Gertrude Jekyll," "William Robinson").

61. Some art historians argue that although Grasset was a major practitioner of art nouveau, he could not have been a major influence on the use of plant designs by other designers because his *La plante et ses applications ornamentales* only began to be published in 1896. But Victor Arwas points out that Grasset's "teaching, counselling, and influencing" of others was under way many years before his own best-known works were published (*Berthon and Grasset* [New York: Rizzoli, 1978], 23, 61; see also 57 and 58 for a discussion of other influential artists using plant forms). Anne Murray-Robertson analyzes Grasset's influence in the United States as well as European countries in *Grasset: Pionnier de l'art nouveau* (Paris: Bibliothèque des Arts Paris, 1981), 200 ff.

62. Murray-Robertson, *Grasset,* 128.

63. Ibid., and see Arwas, *Berthon and Grasset,* 29, for additional illustrations.

64. Carl E. Schorske, *Fin-de-siècle Vienna: Politics and Culture* (New York: Vintage, 1981).

65. David V. Erdman, *The Illuminated Blake: William Blake's Complete Illuminated Works with a Plate-by-Plate Commentary* (New York: Dover, 1974), 33, 34. The obsessive presence of vegetation in the plates can be immediately seen even in collections that contain only a sample of the plates from many works (e.g., Norton Critical Edition, *Blake's Poetry and Designs,* ed. Mary Lynn John-

son and John E. Grant [New York: Norton, 1979]) or which have plates from a single work (see, for example, the 1967 Oxford University Press reproduction of Blake's *Songs of Innocence and of Experience Showing the Two Contrary States of the Human Soul, 1789, 1794,* intro. and commentary by Geoffrey Keynes, which shows the original scale of the small book).

66. Winn, *John Dryden and His World,* 477, 480. Dryden had also translated sections of Ovid's *Metamorphoses* in the previous year (454).

67. Scholars on Shakespeare's flowers often point out that between 1596 and 1604 Shakespeare was living in the neighborhood of Gerard, a famous gardener and author of what is still considered the best-known herbal. The depth of Shakespeare's entanglement with flowers is richly displayed in works such as Rev. Henry N. Ellacombe, *The Plant-Lore and Garden Craft of Shakespeare,* 2d ed. (London, 1884), J. Harvey Bloom, *Shakespeare's Garden* (London: Methuen, 1903), Eleanour Sinclair Rohde, *Shakespeare's Wild Flowers, Fairy Lore, Gardens, Herbs, Gatherers of Simples and Bee Lore* (London: Medici Society, 1935).

68. Though Laertes explicitly identifies violets with Ophelia's body, as Ophelia had earlier allied them with her father's body, he does not explicitly associate their color with her veins. But blue and purple flowers are so allied throughout Shakespeare, both before and after *Hamlet* (1600). "Blue-veined violets" appear in *Venus and Adonis* (1593; line 125); in sonnet 99 (1592–98), Shakespeare adds an extra line to the first quatrain in order to say that the violet attains its saturated color by having been steeped in the beloved's veins (sonnet 99 is the only sonnet Shakespeare has given a surplus line); *A Midsummer Night's Dream* (1594–95) allies the pansy's blue-violet color with mortal blood (II.i.167); and *Cymbeline* (1610) speaks of "the azured harebell, like thy veins" (IV.ii.222).

Throughout this introduction, citations from Shakespeare as well as the specification of dates are from G. B. Harrison, ed., *Shakespeare: The Complete Works* (New York: Harcourt, Brace, 1952).

69. William Shakespeare, *The Tempest* (1611), V.i.88, 89; *Richard II* (1594–95), III.iv.43; *The Tempest,* II.i.90–93.

70. Seamus Heaney, "The Seed Cutters," in *North* (London: Faber and Faber, 1975), 10. Though I am drawing primarily on Heaney's poems of the late eighties and early nineties (*Station Island* [1985], *The Haw Lantern* [1987], *Seeing Things* [1991]), both this poem and the book's title accurately call attention to the fact that reattaching calendar, map, and compass to material grounding has from the very beginning been part of Seamus Heaney's work.

71. Seamus Heaney, "Feeling into Words" (1974), in *Preoccupations: Selected Prose, 1968–1978* (New York: Noonday-Farrar, Straus, and Giroux, 1980), 4,

and Seamus Heaney, "Holly," in *Station Island* (New York: Farrar, Straus, and Giroux, 1985), 85.

72. Seamus Heaney, "The King of the Ditchbacks," in *Station Island* (1985), 57; and see Helen Vendler's account of this poem in "Echo Soundings, Searches, Probes," in *Seamus Heaney,* ed. and intro. Harold Bloom (New Haven: Chelsea, 1986), 171.

73. See, for example, the "dampish feel / Of a clay floor" in the childhood "earth house" whose half door opens "directly into starlight" and thus seems to drop the floor several feet below ground in "Squarings xl," in *Seeing Things* (New York: Farrar, Straus, and Giroux, 1991), 94; so, too, the dormer window in "The King of the Ditchbacks" is positioned below the ground's horizon (57), as is the opening poem of *Station Island,* "The Underground"; see also the extraordinary final paragraph of "The God in the Tree" (1978) in *Preoccupations,* 189, where Heaney emerges from below ground like a plant. The bog poems also belong with these other writings in which Heaney inhabits the ground.

74. Seamus Heaney, "Sweetpea," in *Station Island* (1985), 46, and "Squarings xli," in *Seeing Things* (1991), 95. For the sense that the horizon of ground is at eye level or above, see also "The Mud Vision," in *The Haw Lantern* (New York: Noonday-Farrar, Straus, and Giroux, 1987), 48—

> And then in the foggy midlands it appeared,
> Our mud vision, as if a rose window of mud
> Had invented itself out of the glittery damp,
> A gossamer wheel, concentric with its own hub
> Of nebulous dirt, sullied yet lucent.

—as well as the epigraph to that volume: "The riverbed, dried-up, half-full of leaves. / Us, listening to a river in the trees."

75. Seamus Heaney, "Lightenings vi and vii," in *Seeing Things* (1991), 60, 61, and "The Makings of a Music: Reflections on Wordsworth and Yeats" (1978), in *Preoccupations,* 68. Flowers and plants enter Heaney's descriptions of other poets as well: in his 1992 introduction to Czeslaw Milosz's poetry reading in Cambridge, Ma., Heaney described the heavy blossom of the poem suspended above its stem; and in the essay on Wordsworth and Yeats, he pictures Yeats' poem suspended above the ground ("the voice muscles its way over the obstacle course of the form and flexes like an animated vine on the trellis of its metric and rhyme scheme" [73]). But among Heaney's many portraits of poets, it is Wordsworth and Hardy whose posture in relation to the ground most closely approaches Heaney's own.

76. Eric Partridge, *Origins: A Short Etymological Dictionary of Modern English* (New York: Macmillan, 1966), s.v. "fresh."

77. Ernest Klein, *A Comprehensive Etymological Dictionary of the English Language* (Amsterdam: Elsevier, 1971), s.v. "fresh."

78. As in the phrase "dipingere a fresco" (Partridge, *Origins,* 236).

79. As several of these etymological sources indicate, it is cognate with the word for "sweet" in Old Slavic (*presinu*) and Lithuanian (*prëskas*).

80. Robert K. Barnhart, ed., *The Barnhart Dictionary of Etymology* (New York: H. W. Wilson, 1988), s.v. "fresh."

81. C. T. Onions, ed., *The Oxford Dictionary of English Etymology* (Oxford: Clarendon, 1966), s.v. "fresh."

82. Seamus Heaney, "The Sense of Place" (1977), in *Preoccupations,* 138.

83. Barnhart, *Barnhart Dictionary of Etymology,* s.v. "fresh." Barnhart also observes that "fersch" first appears as "fresh" in 1288 (hence, once more close to the hundred-year mark).

84. S. T. Coleridge, "To William Godwin, September 1800," Letter 75 in *Unpublished Letters of Samuel Taylor Coleridge Including Certain Letters Republished from Original Sources,* ed. Earl Leslie Griggs (New Haven: Yale University Press, 1933), 151.

85. The poetic vow "against our vanishing" first appears in Grossman's poem "Of the Great House," then reappears in the title of Grossman's conversations with Mark Halliday published in *The Sighted Singer.*

86. Mary Lynn Johnson and John E. Grant, editors' introduction to *The Book of Thel,* in *Blake's Poetry and Designs,* 61.

87. William Blake, *The Book of Thel,* part 2, lines 9–10, in *Blake's Poetry and Designs,* 64.

88. W. B. Yeats, *A Vision* (London: Macmillan, 1962), 220.

89. Harrison dates *King John* as 1596 (or between 1589 and 1599), *Richard II* as 1594 or 1595; the *Second Part of Henry IV* as 1598; *Henry V* as 1599; the *Second Part of Henry VI* as between 1590 and 1592; and *Richard III* as 1592 or 1593 (*Shakespeare: The Complete Works,* 541, 430, 653, 732, 142, 221).

90. Yeats, "At Stratford-on-Avon" (1901), 96.

91. W. B. Yeats, "Edmund Spenser" (1902), in *Essays and Introductions,* 382. Yeats says he sometimes thinks this passage "the finest invention of Spenser."

1590s

⚜

Fin-de-Siècle Renaissance England

Margreta de Grazia

As BODIES are dissected, sentences parsed, chemicals broken down, land divided: so too the past is partitioned in order to be understood—into eras, epochs, ages, reigns, periods. The problem then arises of determining where those temporal parts begin and end. The century division would seem the solution with its fixed starting point (A.D. 1) and its clear-cut succession of decimal units. Indeed, it must have seemed so to the first historians to use the century division, the Protestant Magdeburg scholars who in the middle of the sixteenth century began the publication of a church history in sixteen volumes, one volume per century, known as the *Magdeburg Centuries*.[1] Yet even the century division has not been decisive, as is demonstrated by disagreements over, for example, when the nineteenth century really ends and the twentieth begins.[2] Some other principle of division is obviously at work traversing the century's limits, a nonarithmetic principle issuing from within rather than imposed from without—indeed a metaphysical principle that goes by such names as *character, mind-set, temper, worldview, mood, genius,* even *personality,* all of them more or less psychologizing terms apotheosized by Hegel in his account of the "spirit of the age" or *Zeitgeist,* that vast spiritual totality that realizes itself as it unfolds along the historical continuum.

Fin de siècle is a fraction of a century, a century in miniature therefore, but unlike the century it emerged not retrospectively as a way of understanding the bygone past but rather contemporaneously as a way of experiencing the lived present. It was as if the incipient decade, before unfolding in time, had curled itself up in a Victorian easy chair to read Hegel's chiasmatically paired *Philosophy of History* and *History of Philosophy* and precociously assumed an epochal spirit all of its own— or rather an epochal *dis*pirit, a lack of spirit, as if to reject Hegelian history by draining out the very spirit that ran uniformly through it, and by that very negation putting itself in (Hegelian) dialectical relation to it (no escaping Hegel). It was as if the decade wanted to exempt itself from the historical race (and this metaphor is intended to evoke the beginning of the official Olympics in 1896, whose timed races along strictly lined tracks might well emblematize a century of obsessive teleological movement)[3]—a race that it perceived as having already gone too far, surpassing its goal and running itself into the ground, exhausted.

With both of these characterizations of fin de siècle—as impressionable Hegelian reader, as retiring Olympic athlete—I am suggesting that the fin-de-siècle division presupposed a nineteenth-century historiography. The decade gave itself a discrete identity—call it dispirit, malaise, anxiety, fashionable despair—which distinguished it from all other periods while it simultaneously situated itself on the superannuated reaches of the historical continuum. It thus came to possess both a synchronic and diachronic consciousness; in other words, it experienced itself as history or, more precisely, history as defined by the nineteenth century. In this respect fin de siècle is a dated and datable phenomenon: a period piece. In another respect, however, it seems oddly anachronistic. That the late nineteenth century should feel anxiety before the decline of civilization is one thing; that it should connect that anxiety and that decline with the close of century is another. Time, after all, since Leibniz and Kant emptied it of its mystifying presences, remains a neutral, formal receptacle. A secular *siècle* should possess no ominous stretches, no portentous partitions, final or otherwise. The belief that the year's date should even remotely influence the course of history appears as superstitious as believing the day's date, say Friday the thirteenth, brings bad luck, or as credulous as believing a given year, say A.D. 1000, would bring the world to an end. In sum, although the fin de siècle's consciousness of itself as a historical period accords with its time, millenarianism at the onset of the twentieth century appears weirdly anachronistic.

I

It would have been more appropriate at the turn of an earlier century: the sixteenth for example, especially in Elizabethan England, where millenarianism figured centrally in defending the Reformed church against the Catholic, empire against papacy. Through its allegorizing of Revelation, the Reformation pressed eschatology into the service of its own history, making it the driving force behind the temporal ups and downs of its chronic cycles. One need only turn to the book that was chained by official decree in Tudor churches next to the Bishops' Bible to recognize the centrality of the Revelation allegory:[4] John Foxe's 1559 *Acts and Monuments* recorded the cyclical struggle between Christ and Antichrist which would climax apocalyptically with the reign of the second Constantine, the Christian empress Elizabeth.[5] Like any allegory, Revelation also lent itself to seditious readings, and the Crown up to the Civil War attempted to censure readings that subverted rather than sanctioned divine right.[6] As numerous seventeenth-century historians have emphasized, millenarianism played a critical role in instigating and authorizing political change, most dramatically by radical sects such as the Ranters and Diggers, most consequentially by Parliamentarians.[7]

It figured in more specific acts of legitimization as well. The prophecy in Revelation that the end of the world was conditional on the conversion of the Jews and the gathering of the Gentiles was used to defend projects as varied as the burning of witches, New World expansion (some American Indians were considered members of the lost tribes of Israel), commercial contact with the Turks, rampant militancy in Ireland, and various motions to readmit the Jews to England.[8] Another way of establishing the pervasiveness of millenarian thinking would be through literary references, even in Shakespeare alone, not merely because there are so many but because they can be so elliptical and abstract, a tiny hint sufficing to evoke the cataclysmic event (invariably in a periodic syntax that postpones till last the naming of the ultimate): "What, will the line stretch out to th' crack of doom?" "Is

this the Promised End?" "O bloody period," "The rest is silence,"
"And time is at its period."[9] In an apocalyptically minded time, immanent in all endings (syntactic, dramatic, human) was the imminence of
the eschatological end.[10]

Stephen Greenblatt has argued that the manipulation of anxiety was
a key strategy of social control in Renaissance England, in the pulpit, on
the scaffold, and at the theater.[11] If so, it may be because millenarianism
predisposed the period to such a state or "structure of feeling," Raymond Williams' term for the salient feature of an age.[12] As Greenblatt
also notes, there was no need to resort to histrionics to induce anxiety,
for conditions, in the 1590s especially, were of themselves dire enough.
Both historical and literary accounts have represented the decade in
terms of decline which readily lend themselves to fin-de-siècle analysis.
Historians discuss the period as one of crisis; literary historians depict it
as one, if not of decadence, then at least of *disenchantment,* the term
favored in Renaissance anthologies, suggesting that until then Elizabethan England had been under a spell—the spell of an older, more
idealistic time cast by feudalism, hierarchy, community, and ritual, the
salient features of E. M. W. Tillyard's Elizabethan roseate world picture.

Referred to as early as 1926 as "a time of crisis," the 1590s have, in a
recent collection of essays, *The European Crisis of the 1590s,* been considered in specific terms of "*fin de siècle* malaise."[13] The degree of crisis in
England is seen to range, depending on the historian, from "acute
difficulties" to "catastrophic conditions." But the symptoms are fairly
agreed upon: after 1593, there was a series of climatic and agricultural
disasters, bad weather followed by bad harvests, causing corn prices to
as much as treble between 1590 and 1596; poverty and famine ("a
subsistence crisis") ensued, bringing on "endemic social disorder," ag-
gravated by enclosure, high mortality rates (13 percent of London
wiped out by plague in 1593 and 1597), Irish revolts at home (erupting
in Essex's rebellion), the Spanish threat persisting abroad, death taking
its toll among Elizabeth's privy councilors (eleven out of fifteen of
them died in the first six years of the decade), and the queen herself
aging (despite her glamorizing portraits), a particular cause for anxiety
when succession was contested by twelve claimants, exposing England
to the possibility of both internecine strife and foreign invasion.[14]
Economically, politically, and socially, then, the close of the sixteenth

century was a troubled period, "expiring" and "exhausted" like the close of the nineteenth. Yet in modern histories, the end of the sixteenth century is often less important as an autonomous synchronic crisis period than as a critical step in the long diachronic continuum of Western history. Though the precise date is frequently debated, the turn of the sixteenth century often serves to mark nothing less than the "turning point from old to new," more specifically, the shift from feudalism to capitalism, from manor to market, which ushers in the modern age. The arithmetic division between the sixteenth and seventeenth centuries thus nicely coincides with a historical division—*the* major historical division that separates ancient from modern—settling for many what Althusser has called "still the major problem of modern historiography": where to break the historical continuum.[15]

On the literary scene, the troubled symptoms diagnosed by historians find a striking generic correlative in the sudden proliferation of satires and epigrams in that last decade. Literary histories always remark on this short-lived phenomenon during which Elizabethan writers under the auspices of "the cankered muse" railed against social ills, giving poetic and philosophical expression to the lived difficulties I have just itemized from historical accounts.[16] There is no better proof that this satirical outbreak was connected to specific historical grievances than the Crown's reaction in 1599: a crackdown in censorship which called for the banning and burning of satirical works, bringing the genre to an abrupt halt.[17]

But there is another 1590s genre or subgenre that also expresses discontent, in a more private mode. The 1590s were the age of the English sonnet sequence, commencing with the posthumous publication of Sidney's *Astrophil and Stella* in 1591 and ending in the main with Drayton's 1600 *Idea*. About thirty sequences from that decade survive, and undoubtedly many more circulated in manuscript at the time.[18] Shakespeare's Sonnets were published in 1609, but at least some were in circulation in 1598, and all are generally agreed to have been written, if not by 1600, then by 1603.[19] The notion that genres exhaust themselves is particularly interesting in regard to the sonnet, for it *arrived* in England announcing its exhaustion. In the first sonnet of England's sonnet craze, Astrophil refers to his sonnets as posthumous at conception, as "Petrarch's long-deceased woes," and Shakespeare fears that present verse teems with life already born, bearing "the second burthen of a former child" (59).

Nearly dead on arrival, sonnets keep reproducing themselves all the same: not singly, not in scores, but by the hundreds. Modern criticism has accounted for their numbers by regarding them as literary exercises repeated in order to attain and display virtuosity, as if the only reason to repeat a form were to perfect it. But I would like to suggest that these runs of English sonnets represent what cannot be perfected, perfected in the Renaissance sense of brought to completion. Their content is chronic discontent. The form repeats itself because the desire it articulates, be it erotic, political, artistic, can never be satisfied. The poet becomes synonymous with desire—Shakespeare's "my name is *Will*"; indeed, sonnets are called "aymes," reducing the first person, in the grammatical position of both subject (I) and object (me), to that longing cry, the perfect autoreferential utterance. Rather than ending, the sonnets just stop coming, and even then not always conclusively. A number of sonnet sequences (Shakespeare's among them) are followed by anacreontics and complaints that move perversely backward into mythic and historical time as if to mock the possibility of futurity.[20] Stuck in desire, stuck in the past, they can only repeat what was always already repetition, without changing or concluding. (The term *sequence* has been misleading, suggesting the very continuity and progression sonnets so conspicuously lack. It should be no surprise that it emerged in the late nineteenth century in an edition of Shakespeare's Sonnets by Edward Dowden, who also "sequenced" Shakespeare's life and works along a developmental chronological trajectory—another Hegelian inspiration.)[21]

If sonnets are literary exercises, they are of a Sisyphean or Tantalean kind, which undo themselves in the doing, exercises in futility or prolonged longing: "Had, having, in quest to have extreme." As has been noted, all sonnet sequences (with the exception of Spenser's *Amoretti*) end in despair, a foregone conclusion or inconclusion, a 1590s or golden age version of the 1890s or Gilded Age malaise, a lack of hope (de-*sperare*) in the possibility of change which Jonathan Dollimore discusses in a recent essay as death-encoded desire, an Elizabethan anticipation of Freud's Victorian death wish.[22] One of the great critical challenges has been to find change within these compulsively repetitive runs of sonnets that themselves dwell constantly on mutability. But one has to question the search for development—of narrative, theme, character—in a convention that is programmatically monotonous, one that strings out sonnet after sonnet like Macbeth's undifferentiated tomorrows and tomorrows and tomorrows that dead-end in dusty death.

As the national crisis of the 1590s draws feudalism to a close, so too the sonnets signal the end of an era, what one critic has termed the "last decadent flickers" of the Petrarchan tradition. As historically experienced discontent heralds the beginning of capitalism, so too aesthetically expressed discontent marks a not unrelated development: the emergence of individualism. Though a recent study on Renaissance periodization refers to Petrarchism as the style in which "Renaissance individualism chooses to fall in love,"[23] critical consensus (in regard to the English sequences at least) suggests otherwise: that individualism left the form behind. Even the most valued sonnets have been considered too trapped in imitation, convention, and tradition to allow for personal individuation. J. W. Lever's thesis of 1956 has more or less held: the English sonneteers failed, in his mind, to break out of the Petrarchan schema into something genuinely new until, of course, Shakespeare.[24] Indeed, it is an unexpectedly smooth generational skip from J. W. Lever in 1956 to Joel Fineman in 1986, who identifies the pre-Shakespearean sonneteers with the traditional specular idealism that he sees Shakespeare as having effectively disrupted with novel verbal duplicity, thereby adding to his myriad accomplishments "the invention of poetic subjectivity," the subtitle of Fineman's book.[25] Though the terms are strangely Lacanian, the narrative is quite familiar: Shakespeare, as watershed figure, marks the shift, if not from convention to originality or from old to new, then from the Imaginary to the Symbolic, from old-fashioned identity to modern subjectivity. Indeed, the break between the two segments of the sonnets (as the beloved changes from fair youth to dark lady) looks in Fineman's account like the turn of the century itself: the turn from sonnet 126 to sonnet 127 marks the rupturing of the Imaginary by the Symbolic, which ushers in what Fineman calls "an epoch of subjectivity" which stretches all the way from Shakespeare through Freud.[26]

Just as social crisis leads to a long history of capitalism, so its literary analogue sets off a long narrative of subjectivity. And Shakespeare's career has since Dowden (1875) followed a similar trajectory known as authorial development, from "apprentice" to "master-dramatist," from immature comic to mature tragic works, with *Hamlet* (usually dated 1600–1601) marking the transition midway.[27] Conveniently at the century's break, Shakespeare's career breaks in half, just at the juncture where, in the political realm, old gives way to new. In some readings, the turn of the century, the high point of Shakespeare's career, and the golden age of English poetry all coincide: the " 'Shakespearean moment,' the opening years of the seventeenth century, in which were written all the supreme Shakespearean dramas."[28] The end of the sixteenth century, then, has become an important turning point in three coordinate histories (of early capitalism, subjectivity, and authorial genius), possessing both the synchronic coherence and the diachronic telos that nineteenth-century historiography requires.[29]

II

I hope my sketch of the 1590s at the level of the historical and cultural suffices to qualify them for fin-de-siècle status. As I also pointed out, their eschatological consciousness further contributed to a fin-de-siècle spirit, or anxious *dis*pirit. But—and here I announce my *own* turning point—the 1590s could not possibly, NOT IN A MILLION YEARS, have given even a thought to the end of the century. And for a very simple reason. There was no such thing as a century in the 1590s, or at least not one that referred specifically to a hundred *years*. In what *we* term the sixteenth century, *century* was a collective noun referring to a hundred similar things. It could be a military unit, like the subdivision of a Roman legion: Cordelia bids that "a century" be sent forth to find Lear (as if to compensate for his disbanded knights). But its primary use seems to have been as a classification for textual materials: there are centuries of ballads, centuries of prayers, centuries of stories, centuries of poems, as in such familiar Elizabethan titles as Thomas Watson's *Hekatompathia or passionate Centurie of love* (1582) or Barnaby Barnes' *A divine Centurie of Spirituall Sonnets* (1595).[30] Though historians have not noted this, it is as a bibliographic classification that the word first appeared in relation to history: when the Magdeburg Centuriators, the Protestant historians I have already mentioned, assigned one volume to each one hundred years of church history, "century" was still a bibliographic rather than a temporal unit. It is not until the eighteenth century that "century" rather than "century of years" designated a temporal unit exclusively.

In his bold and intriguing recent book on historical periodization, *Trahir le temps,* the French-Israeli historian Daniel Milo makes the astonishing claim, "La révolution 'créa' le siècle."[31] It took an event as cataclysmic as the French Revolution, he argues, to cut the present off from the past, definitively and conclusively. With all ties to the present severed, the past became a closed book, as it were, divisible into hundred-year chapters. Both time and space in republican France were reformed on a decimal base: a ten-month year, ten-day week, a ten-hour day, a hundred-minute hour, a hundred-second minute; and space was simultaneously decimalized by the metric system. As Milo points out through an examination of titles before and after the French Revolution, "*le siècle*" became the standard historical unit only after the 1790s. And without a *siècle* there could be, of course, no *fin de siècle.* Indeed, it took more than an earthshaking—earth-*rending*—event to produce that phenomenon: the event had to coincide with the end of the (newly delineated) century, what Milo wryly terms "l'heureuse coincidence de la Fin d'un Monde et de la Fin d'un Siècle." Thus 1890 was the very earliest that fin-de-siècle malaise could be experienced, the first centennial of the Revolution, recalling its massive upheavals, stirring up a subliminal anticipation that things once again might change or cease. In sum, according to Milo, there could be no fin de siècle until *after* 1790 not only because time was not yet measured in centurial units but because nothing as portentous as the French Revolution had yet occurred at the end of a century to riddle subsequent ones with anxiety. The subsequent century remembered that trauma at its own conclusion, and so too may our own, unless we repress our historical memory altogether (and such repressions are, it has been said, characteristic of our age).

Perhaps a hundredfold: we in the 1990s are approaching not only the end of a century but the end of a millennium. Clearly millennial anxiety is older than secular, dating back to the prophetic books of Daniel and Saint John. It must be added, however, that the Bible specifies no point at which to start counting to A.D. 1000. As Milo notes, even the decision to start counting time itself from the Nativity was somewhat arbitrary (indeed, it did not become usual until the eighth century).[32] Why not begin with the creation of the world, or with Mohammed's flight from Mecca to Medina? Or, to stay within Christian parameters (and that is *all* they are), why not start earlier, with the Annunciation, or later, with the Crucifixion—as Milo does for experiment's sake, by reorganizing the past into centuries with all dates set back thirty-three years? (The twentieth century looks particularly odd with no World War I, no Proust, no Russian Revolution, no cubism, no silent film, indeed no modernism.) Similarly there was no fixed point from which to start counting to the millennial 1000: the conversion of Constantine was a possibility, but so too were the instauration of the pope, the destruction of the Temple of Jerusalem, the advent of Julian the Apostate—and in every case, there was disagreement about the date of those events as well.[33] Furthermore, there was always the possibility that any calculation betrayed a literal or carnal understanding of what the Bible intended figuratively or spiritually, as Augustine influentially maintained in *City of God*.

What is to be said, then, about the year A.D. 1000, when "a general consternation seized mankind; [when] many relinquished their possessions, and abandoning their friends and families, hurried with precipitation to the Holy Land, where they imagined that Christ would quickly appear to judge the world"? These are the words of the Scottish historian William Robertson in 1769.[34] As prominent medievalists have been arguing for more than a century, however, nothing of the sort happened in the year 1000.[35] There is no evidence that there was any particular consternation around that year; it is not even clear that there was much awareness of what year it was (whether it was 998 or 999) at a time in which it was the natural seasons and the liturgical calendar that counted. Robertson's reason for identifying medieval Europe with such credulity (and it is an identification from which the field of medieval studies still suffers) can be gleaned from the title of the preface in which the passage appears: "A view of the *progress* of society in Europe." This view does not become legendary, however, until Jules Michelet's *Histoire de France* (1833–62), in which A.D. 1000 figures not only as the low point of Christian ignorance and barbarity but also (and very movingly in Michelet) as the premature point of a pathetically misdirected search for truth in Christian Revelation which would not be found until France's Revolution.[36]

Thus our most common and obvious way of measuring time, in terms of decades, centuries, and millennia, was a revolutionary development, and a relatively recent one—only two centuries old. This is not to suggest the absurd: that history was not previously divided. There have always been eras, ages, epochs, times, reigns, but they were not arithmetically determined. Other period divisions were based on religious or political considerations. Histories were divided into six ages because God took that many days to create, or into four monarchies because there were that many in Daniel's prophecy, or three eras representing times before, under, and after the Law, or (returning to John Foxe's *Acts and Monuments*) into five cycles enacting the struggle between Christ and Antichrist. Alternatively, histories, such as Holinshed's 1577 *Chronicles,* were divided into the reigns of monarchs, already a move toward the secularization of time, as the state rather than the church became the principle by which time was organized. As is evinced by the examples of imperial Rome and postrevolutionary regimes such as those of France, China, and the Soviet Union, to encode a regime in time—historical and calendric—is a powerful way of punctuating memory and experience, public and private.[37] It was to resist papal domination that England held fast to the increasingly discrepant Julian calendar until 1751 (when the solar year lagged thirteen days behind the Old Style calendric year) rather than submit to the pope's reformed Gregorian calendar available as early as 1582.

III

Unlike Christian eras and imperial reigns, the arithmetic century division should be neutral, as devoid of ideological inscriptions as number itself. There seems to be something of a confusion, then, in the fin de siècle's conflation of the end of the century with the decline of civilization, its linking of a neutral temporal division with either apocalyptic ruin or revolutionary upheaval. Century marks were never particularly favored in millenarian predictions, which more commonly fell on irregular years: 1523, 1588, 1607, 1656, and so on. And it seems poignantly ironic that the French Revolution, after having mobilized the desacralizing ideas of the Enlightenment, should return to haunt future centuries with its own foreboding memory. It may be that we need to turn to another science to explain that declining hundred-year span, not to medieval divine eschatology or modern secular history but rather to human biology.

A century corresponds to a superannuated life span, a very long human life. Yet perhaps biology is not the right science either, since a period is never imagined as possessing a characteristic physiology—a *body* or an *anatomy*[38]—but rather a distinctive spirit, mind, genius, character, temper, personality even. We might then have to shift into psychology, in which case the fin de siècle could be seen to have further individuated the anthropomorphic senescent century with an illness, not a physiological but a psychological one—anxiety, a disease or unease of the mind, or more accurately of the nervous system, a nervous disorder, then, a neurosis just short of hysteria. And if it is indeed the case that the decade was not so bad after all—as some recent studies have emphasized by drawing attention to such positive changes as quantum mechanics, mass politics, the diffusion of culture and literacy, and most dramatically the generation and distribution of electrical energy—it was all, then, in the patient's mind, suggesting that our retiring, precocious fin-de-siècle reader had also perused Freud (very early Freud) before contracting a psychoanalyzable neurosis as its distinguishing periodic feature, thereby applying the finishing touches on a fully personified century.[39]

As it turns out, however, they were not the *final* finishing touches, for the end of the twentieth century seems to have come up with another disorder, schizophrenia, a psychic rather than a nervous disorder, as if it had been reading not (or not only) Hegel and Freud but [Nietzschean] Foucault and [Lacanian] Deleuze. Repeatedly evoked to describe a range of contemporary cultural phenomena, schizophrenia is best understood in linguistic terms as a snapping of the signifying chain that relates words in sense-making sequences.[40] With syntax shattered, only scattered textual bits and pieces (signifieds) remain. Schizophrenia shatters that other form of syntagmatic continuity as well—history—leaving behind scattered temporal bits and pieces (immediacies). I'm not sure whether one can still think of the century in human terms—*humanoid*, perhaps—for schizophrenic language, memory, and feeling are transformed beyond recognition. In all events, like a good reader still, the decade continues to keep up with the times, though it is hard to know what that phrase could possibly mean when time is experienced as fragmented immediacies, as so many disjunctive and isolated presents.

But I've rushed ahead of myself here and wish to return to the nineteenth century when the inanimate century started (pathetically) assuming human traits. It is tempting to see this historiographic transformation in the context of what Foucault has termed "the epistemological mutation of history" which undermined the sovereignty of the subject.[41] Disciplines that once upheld the subject's centrality—in particular, ethnology, linguistics, and psychoanalysis—now threatened it by unfixing its social structures, unhinging its linguistic rules, and unfastening its constitutive desires and sexuality. It was in Foucault's account in defensive response to this conceptual upheaval that history was cast as one protracted "history of consciousness," a long progressive Hegelian unfolding of the human spirit. (Each of the three parallel narratives by which the 1590s have here been represented belong to this history.) Continuous history served as the commodious "abode" or "shelter" for the embattled sovereign subject, holding out the hope of its reinstatement, the promise "that one day the subject—in the form of historical consciousness—will once again be able to . . . bring back under [its] sway all those things that are kept at a distance by difference." What could be more enabling to such a project than a psychologized century, one made in the very image of the heroes, great men, and geniuses whose trajectories it privileged, a transposition of the pathetic fallacy from nature onto Time? It is this perfectly sympathetic fit that is reflected in the fin de siècle's act of self-definition, for the very term designated from the start both a personal mood and a temporal modality, as in one of its earliest (1886) formulations: "to be *fin de siècle* . . . is to languish with one's century, to decay along with it."[42]

IV

Perhaps there has always been a need to anthropomorphize time, as if in human form it might become somehow negotiable. In the form of Father Time, time can be challenged, even in hand-to-hand combat, as when Shakespeare pits his incisive stylus against Time's cutting scythe, "all in war with Time" (sonnet 15).[43] It may be that the need to humanize time was even more acutely felt with the invention of the mechanical clock, making it necessary to cover up its relentless wheels and gears with a friendly watching face, two moving hands, and enough language to tell time. For the same reason, perhaps, the bell clapper was transformed into a personable *jacquemart* or just plain Jack, a jack-of-all-trades or common handyman hammering out time on an anvil. Timepieces could also be personalized with the insignias of their owner—portraits, monograms, mottos—which like good trademarks were both ornamental and proprietary. Without need for sun to show time, for bells to toll time, an owner, holding, pocketing, consulting his timepiece at will, might imagine that not just the timepiece but time itself belonged to him, as if he were time's keeper, proprietor of what once was as much a common good as the sun or the church steeple or the civic tower. The profoundly antisocial nature of that illusion can be gauged by comparing Donne's expansive response to the tolling of communal bells—"I am involved in mankind"[44]—with the still current expression for the ultimate in selfishness, "He wouldn't give you the time of day." In removing the individual from communal dependencies the private clock functioned like that other early modern vade mecum, the book, which gave solitary access to words just as *the* book or Bible gave solitary access to the word of God. It is worth remarking that these two alienable and alienating objects, clocks and Bibles, were both specifically Protestant developments, instrumental in the cultivation of that quiet interiority so often ascribed to the Reformation, as if the owner's intimacy with these two objects led to their internalization as internal clock and inner consciousness respectively.

And yet there is much in the period working to keep time impersonal. Birthdays were not celebrated in the Renaissance or even generally recorded, leaving subsequent centuries guessing at the birthdays of even the most famous. It was the day of baptism which was recorded in the parish register when an infant was named and admitted into the body of the church.[45] The only claim an individual had to a place on the calendar was through his or her namesake, commonly the saint whose day was frequently highlighted by red letters on the liturgical calendar. Birthdays were considered pagan rituals that slighted the only birthday that counted, the Nativity of Christ. It was from that birth that time itself began to be counted. *Anno Domini,* A.D., in the year of our Lord: customarily accompanied the date, as if to keep time from going secular by reinscribing its Christological origin. Even Samuel Pepys, in a diary so private that it is written in secret code, prefaced his entries with that citation, as if to situate his quotidian days in relation to that momentous year.

One person *was* annually celebrated, though not on her birthday. The queen was honored on Accession Day, the day on which she assumed the identity of head of church and state. It was from that point that legal documents and statutes were dated—for example, 49 H. 3 (the forty-ninth year of the reign of Henry III) or 1265—and the royal sponsorship of all new legislation thereby registered. Yet there were limits even to the sovereign's authority over time. Extending only as far back into the past as the written record and chronicles, royalty was superceded by an older institution: the Ancient Constitution. In arguing for the constitution's inviolability, common-law lawyers appealed to its existence since "time out of mind" or "time immemorial"; according to J. G. A. Pocock, "belief in an immemorial law . . . was a nearly universal belief of Englishmen" until well after the English Revolution.[46] Originating in a time before human agency of any kind had left its mark—before any monarch, before any legislator—the constitution survived through custom rather than, like civil and canon law, through writ. It was the law of the land which ruled over property and its inheritance, prior to and therefore free from royal prerogative. In *Richard II* (1594–95), this law is defended as Time's "customary rights," precisely the rights King Richard tries to take from Time by denying Bullingbrook his father's land and titles, a denial that blocks temporal succession ("Let not to-morrow then ensue to-day") as well as the kingship that depends on it ("Be not thyself" [II.i.196, 197–98]). For his presumption, Richard in the final act is turned into a surrealistic "numb'ring clock" whose "sighs, tears, and groans/Show minutes, times, and hours" (V.vi.57–58):

> For now hath time made me his numb'ring clock:
> My thoughts are minutes, and with sighs they jar
> Their watches on unto mine eyes, the outward watch,
> Whereto my finger, like a dial's point,
> Is pointing still, in cleansing them from tears.

Now, sir, the sound that tells what hour it is
Are clamorous groans, which strike upon my heart,
Which is the bell.

(51–57)

From autocrat to automaton: for willfully taking time into his own hands he himself is reduced to the involuntary motion of clockwork.[47]

Sighs, groans, and tears recall the "aymes" or sonnets of the 1590s, ticking off time in measured fourteen-line sounds, the word *sonnet* itself derived from *sonnetto,* or "small sound." It is because sonnets come as regularly and predictably as clockwork that they have been disparaged as mere mechanical exercises. But their relation to time has a grander origin, in the model of all English sonnet collections. Petrarch's *Canzoniere* consists of 366 poems in which three years from Petrarch's singular life—1327 (his first sight of Laura), 1341 (his coronation as poet laureate), and 1347 (the death of Laura)—uneasily intersect with the liturgical year in a basically chiasmic fashion, so that the birth of his love for Laura coincides with Christ's Crucifixion, and Laura's death (264 days and poems later) coincides with Christ's Nativity.[48] Petrarch's personal time thus complexly plays off the liturgical year in an attempt to synchronize his laureate passion and his passion for Laura with Christ's sacrificial passion. Shakespeare also begins marking time from the first sight of his beloved in sonnet 104, counting up three years from "when first your eye I eye'd," a phrase whose repetitions translate into sound the visual mirroring of the poet's "I" in his beloved's "eye," narcissism's solipsistic gaze that sees itself even in the beloved.

Petrarch's precedent has driven modern scholars to look for numerological patterns in his English successors, with questionable results in Shakespeare but with undeniable success in Spenser's *Amoretti*.[49] Set against a backdrop of holy days and seasons, the sonnets record events in Spenser's life, an ample number beginning "One day," "This day," "Dayly." But there is nothing to commemorate in any of these days except another stage of Spenser's "long while" or "Long languishing," of his relentless offensive "incessant battery" (sonnet XIV) and his mistress's relentless defensive "incessant battry" (sonnet LVII), a long record of vain activity—fabrics spun to be unwoven (sonnet XXIII), pages written to be burned (sonnet XLVIII), writing on the shore effaced by the tide, written again and effaced again (sonnet LVII).[50] But the futility ends in the triumphant rhythms of the marriage song or *Epithalamion* (published with *Amoretti* in 1595), a poem consisting of 365 "long lines" and twenty-four stanzas (each rounded off with a refrain worded positively in sixteen stanzas and negatively in eight to differentiate hours of light and darkness at the summer solstice).[51] Once aligned with natural and social rhythms, time breaks out of its personalized syndrome and advances toward a generational and salvational future.

As mentioned earlier, Spenser's are the only sonnets that do not end in despair, unlike Shakespeare's that remain in the rut of "Had, having, and in quest to have" (sonnet 129), the chronic fever "longing still / For that which longer nurseth the disease": "Desire is death" (sonnet 147). In its rawest form, that drive is lust, whose ability to take over time is represented in *Romeo and Juliet* (1594) by a sexualized clock: "The bawdy hand of the dial is now upon the prick of noon" (II.iv.112–13), the high noon of erection which in sonnet 151 dares to pattern itself on the Resurrection, the climax of the Christian year.[52] This bawdy clock brings another "Jack of the clock" to mind—Jack Falstaff, who needs a custom-made timepiece in order to measure his massively self-indulgent life. To him, ordinary time is of no relevance, as Prince Hal points out in response to Falstaff's opening question, "Now, Hal, what time of day is it, lad?"

> Prince. What the devil hast thou to do with the time of the day? unless hours were cups of sack, and minutes capons, and clocks the tongues of bawds, and dials the signs of leaping-houses, and the blessed sun himself a fair hot wench in flame-color'd taffeta? (*First Part of Henry IV* [1597], I.i.6–10)

Catered to his riotous appetites, Falstaff's clock runs increasingly counter(clockwise) to the historical time of Tudor ideology which ultimately motivates Hal.

It is surprising to find a similarly personalized horological configuration in one of the most lyrical of Shakespeare's Sonnets, sonnet 73, in which Shakespeare turns himself into not a clock but a calendar or book of hours.

That time of year thou mayst in me behold
When yellow leaves, or none, or few, do hang
Upon those boughs which shake against the cold,
Bare [ruin'd] choirs, where late the sweet birds sang.
In me thou seest the twilight of such day
As after sunset fadeth in the west,
Which by and by black night doth take away,
Death's second self, that seals up all in rest.
In me thou seest the glowing of such fire
That on the ashes of his youth doth lie,
As the death-bed whereon it must expire,
Consum'd with that which it was nourish'd by.
    This thou perceiv'st, which makes thy love more strong,
    To love that well, which thou must leave ere long.

Although books of hours typically illustrate the changing seasons in images of ritualized collective activity, Shakespeare represents them *in himself,* as is underscored by the thrice-repeated "in me." From that narrow perspective, the passing of time can be experienced only negatively, as bereavement. Everything is taken away—green leaves, bird song, daylight, glowing fire—as if irretrievably. The sonnet is about leave-taking, beginning in leaves falling and ending in beloved leaving, not exactly a valediction, since everything leaves (or is about to leave) *him,* including his beloved, unexpectedly because it is he himself whom death is on the verge of taking away.[53] And yet the shift in the poem from one site to another poignantly suggests the search for another focus. Retreating from cold and dark, Shakespeare moves from one gathering place to another, as if looking for company: from communal church to domestic hearth, both abandoned.[54] Excluding and excluded from the participatory energies that assure cyclical recurrence, the sonnet is a defective book of hours that ends up in the couplet seizing the little that remains—or exhorting his beloved to do so—not because what remains is at its prime but because it is on its "death-bed," a *carpe diem* logic urged with *contemptus mundi* rhetoric. Shakespeare bereaved, Richard deposed, Falstaff banished: each one estranged in an eccentric time, which a later romanticism and lyricism will richly compensate with subjectivity and even genius.

THIS CHAPTER began by illustrating how nicely—too nicely—the 1590s can be made to conform with fin-de-siècle periodization, but ever since its announced turning point, it has done nothing but discredit periodization as peculiar to the nineteenth century and alien to the sixteenth. In this respect, it has itself been true to the times, for periodization has become somewhat unfashionable. This was not always the case: in the 1940s and 1950s, it was one of the liveliest topics in literary criticism (as well as art history), especially in respect to the Renaissance and romanticism.[55] Still testifying to their power are our institutional and pedagogical structures, all organized by historical periods: curricula, syllabi, textbooks, journals, departments, conferences. While still working within these periodic structures, criticism now tends to avoid periodization, in part because of structuralism's focus on synchrony rather than diachrony, on systems rather than development—reflected, for example, in New Historicism's tendency to move *across* time through static homologies rather than *through* time via dynamic change and development.[56] But there are also ideological reasons for its current disfavor. At a time when "totality" in any form is mistrusted, there is little interest in historical structures that unify activity around a single notion—a Kantian "regulative idea" or a Jamesonian "cultural dominant," two terms that raise the queasy suspicion that conceptual totalities might be the instruments of political totalitarianism.[57] In addition, once these totalizing periodic structures are situated on the historical continuum, they encourage any number of suspect narratives: of progress, geneticism, and evolution. It is the study of non-Western cultures which stands to lose most: to cast, for example, postcolonial studies into a sequential and progressive history (of its own or of the West) thrusts its subjects back into the imperialist ideology they have (as the prefix *post-* asserts) left behind.[58] In both its synchronic and diachronic forms, then, periodization is suspected of occluding difference: excluding it from or absorbing it into hegemonic wholes, casting it by the wayside of its streamlined trajectory. We trust in fragments now instead of in wholes, in sites of dispersal rather than in continuous movement, in Nietzschean genealogies or Foucaultian archaeologies rather than in Hegelian teleology.[59]

AND YET, at the same time that periodization has become unfashionable in studying the past, it is all the rage in studying the present.

The mere face that the term *postmodernism* has caught on with such rapidity in the realms of the academic and mediatic is itself indicative of a contemporary eagerness to periodize, not the past but the present. Though there may no longer be an interest in what constitutes and causes a break between one period and the next, what characterizes the spans between the breaks, how those spans relate to one another along the historical continuum, there is an intense interest in talking about what makes (or does not make) the *present* postmodern. This gives a curious twist to the "loss of historicity" that is repeatedly singled out as the dominant trait of the present age. Why is the age talking about itself as a period if it has no sense of history? It is a compelling contradiction, I think, implicit in the first sentence of Frederic Jameson's *Postmodernism, or the Logic of Late Capitalism:* "It is safest to grasp the concept of postmodern as an attempt to think the present historically in an age that has forgotten how to think historically in the first place." The age wants *irrepressibly* to think historically, but it has *repressed* the means by which to do so. Yet this diagnosis too is framed in the psychologizing terms—denial, repression, the unconscious—which, as this chapter has argued, are peculiar to the modern period. It seems strange that the cultural critic most eager to push the age out of modernism's obsession with monadic individualism should have recourse to humanizing terms in discussing temporal divisions. Should not psychologized historical periods fall under Jameson's general indictment of modernism's disabling effect: "a humanization of the world goes hand in hand with a spreading of philosophic and existential despair"?[60] Why are history's subjectifying projections exempt from this critique? Perhaps their lingering presence is a sign that we are still after all only postmodern and not yet something else entirely beyond that.

NOTES

1. On the Magdeburg Centuriators, who between 1559 and 1574 published thirteen of the projected sixteen volumes, see Hillel Schwartz, *Century's End: A Cultural History of the Fin de Siècle from the 990s through the 1990s* (New York: Doubleday, 1990), 93, and Daniel S. Milo, *Trahir le temps (histoire)* (Paris: Les Belles Lettres, 1991), 68–70.

2. For two extremes of centurial flexibility, compare Immanuel Waller-

stein's "long seventeenth century" (1600–1750) in *The Modern World-System II: Mercantilism and the Consolidation of the European World-Economy* (New York: Academic Press, 1974), 8, with Frederic Jameson's account of "the brief 'American century' (1945–73)" in *Postmodernism, or, The Cultural Logic of Late Capitalism* (Durham, N.C.: Duke University Press, 1991), xx. Similar liberties are taken with the boundaries of the decade, as in Jameson's discussion of the sixties which begins in 1967 and ends in 1974, "Periodizing the Sixties," in *The Ideologies of Theory Essays, 1971–1986,* vol. 2 (Minneapolis: University of Minnesota Press, 1988), esp. 204–5. See also Fernand Braudel's discussion "of the very long time span, of the *longue durée,*" and the very "short time span" of a *"nouvelle sonnante"* in *On History,* trans. Sarah Matthews (Chicago: University of Chicago Press, 1980), 25–54.

3. Henning Eichberg, "Forward Race and the Laughter of Pygmies: On Olympic Sport," in *Fin de Siècle and Its Legacy,* ed. Mikulas Teich and Roy Porter (Cambridge: Cambridge University Press, 1990), 115–31.

4. On the chaining of these two books (along with John Jewel's *Defence of the Apology of the Church of England* and Erasmus's *Paraphrases*), see William M. Lamont, *Godly Rule: Politics and Religion, 1603–1660* (London: Macmillan, 1969), 34.

5. See Frances A. Yates, *Astrae: The Imperial Theme in the Sixteenth Century* (London: Routledge and Kegan Paul, 1975), 42–50.

6. See Christopher Hill, " 'Till the Conversion of the Jews,' " in *The Collected Essays* (Amherst: University of Massachusetts Press, 1986), 2:269–300.

7. On the relation between millenarianism and political revolution generally, see Norman Cohn, *The Pursuit of the Millennium* (New York: Harper Torchbooks, 1957); and in the seventeenth century, see Lamont, *Godly Rule.*

8. On the messianism link to witch-hunting, see H. R. Trevor-Roper, *The European Witch-Craze of the Sixteenth and Seventeenth Centuries, and Other Essays* (New York: Harper Torchbooks, 1976), 90–192; on its link to anti-Semitism, see Hill, " 'Till the Conversion of the Jews,' " 269–300.

9. *Macbeth* (I.vi.117), *King Lear* (V.iii.264), *Othello* (V.ii.356), *Hamlet* (V.ii.358), and *Antony and Cleopatra* (IV.xiv.107), in *The Riverside Shakespeare,* gen. ed. G. Blakemore Evans (Boston: Houghton Mifflin, 1974). All subsequent citations from Shakespeare follow this edition and appear parenthetically in text.

10. Frank Kermode argues that concern with "the end" shifts around the time of the Reformation, from Apocalypse (in which cosmic destruction is historically imminent) to tragedy (in which individual death is fictionally immanent). See *The Sense of an Ending: Studies in the Theory of Fiction* (New York: Oxford University Press, 1968), esp. 27–28.

11. See Stephen Greenblatt, "Martial Law in the Land of Cockaigne," in *Shakespearean Negotiations: The Circulation of Social Energy in Renaissance England* (Berkeley and Los Angeles: University of California Press, 1988), esp. 137–38. See also William Bouwsma's chapter "Calvin's Anxiety"—"Nothing bound Calvin more closely to his time than his anxiety"—in *John Calvin: A Sixteenth Century Portrait* (New York: Oxford University Press, 1988), 32. *Anxiety* is a key term in periodizing the modern period as well as the early modern, as in Frederic Jameson's diagnosis of "historical pathology" from romantic *despair* to Victorian *ennui* to modern *anxiety*, each state a particular psychic adaptation to the historical process in which the world falls increasingly under human control ("The Vanishing Mediator," in *Ideologies of Theory Essays*, vol. 2, esp. 6–10). It is also a key term in marking the shift to the postmodern—"Concepts such as anxiety and alienation . . . are no longer appropriate in the world of the postmodern," which is characterized by "not merely a liberation from anxiety but a liberation from every other kind of feeling as well" (*Postmodernism*, 14, 15).

12. For Williams' differentiation of generations or periods by "structures of *feeling*" and "structures of *experience*," see "Structures of Feeling," in *Marxism and Literature* (Oxford: Oxford University Press, 1992), 128–41.

13. J. H. Elliott, "Yet Another Crisis?" in *The European Crisis of the 1590s*, ed. Peter Clark (London: George Allen and Unwin, 1985), 301.

14. These details were culled from the following essays in *The European Crisis of the 1590s:* Peter Clark, introduction, 1–22; R. B. Outhwaite, "Dearth, the English Crown, and the 'Crisis of the 1590s,'" 23–43; C. S. L. Davies, "Popular Disorder," 244–60; and J. H. Elliott, "Yet Another Crisis?" 301–12.

15. Louis Althusser and Étienne Balibar, *Reading Capital*, trans. Ben Brewster (London: Verso, 1979), 94. See also Michel de Certeau's account of how modern Western history begins with a "breakage" between present and past which gets "everywhere" repeated in a chronology of periods (*The Writing of History* [New York: Columbia University Press, 1988], 2).

16. "Usury, rack-renting, land enclosures, the growth of London, soldiers discharged from the Lowland wars, and the vast increase of personal fortunes are all dealt with in both the satires of the time and in various nonliterary documents such as petitions to the Crown and acts of Parliament" (Alvin Kernan, *The Cankered Muse: Satire of the English Renaissance* [New Haven: Yale University Press, 1959], 39). Jonathan Crewe, following Hayden White's identification of historical periods with literary genres, urges that the Renaissance be identified with satire rather than romance (*Trials of Authorship: Anterior Forms and Poetic Reconstruction from Wyatt to Shakespeare* [Berkeley and Los Angeles: University of California Press, 1990], 5–10).

17. See Richard A. McCabe, "Elizabethan Satire and the Bishops' Ban of 1599," *Yearbook of English Studies* 11 (1981), 188–93.

18. Arthur Marotti discusses the coinciding of the sonnet craze with the final years of Elizabeth's reign in " 'Love Is Not Love': Elizabethan Sonnet Sequences and the Social Order," *English Literary History* 49 (1982), 396–428.

19. Sonnet 107 figures as a crucial document in determining the date when the Sonnets were written, though the date when "[t]he mortal moon hath her eclipse endured" ranges widely, from 1588 Armada to 1603 Death of Elizabeth. See *The Sonnets and a Lover's Complaint,* ed. John Kerrigan (Harmondsworth, Middlesex: Penguin, 1986), 313–20.

20. See Katherine Duncan-Jones, "Was the 1609 *Shake-speares Sonnets* Really Unauthorized?" *Renaissance English Studies* 34 (1983), 151–71.

21. Thomas P. Roche, Jr., mentions the term's anachronicity in *Petrarch and the English Sonnet Sequences* (New York: AMS Press, 1989), xi–xii. For Dowden's application of the term, see *The Sonnets of William Shakspere* (London, 1881); for his account of Shakespeare's sequential development, see *A Shakspere Primer* (New York, 1877); *Shakspere: A Critical Study of His Mind and Art* (1874; London: Routledge and Kegan Paul, 1967); and *Introduction to Shakspere* (London, 1893).

22. Jonathan Dollimore, "Desire Is Death," in *Object and Subject: Reconstructing Renaissance Culture,* ed. Margreta de Grazia, Maureen Quilligan, and Peter Stallybrass (Cambridge: Cambridge Univ. Press, forthcoming).

23. See William Kerrigan and Gordon Braden, *The Idea of the Renaissance* (Baltimore: Johns Hopkins University Press, 1989), 159.

24. J. W. Lever, *The Elizabethan Love Sonnet* (London: Methuen, 1956), esp. 160–61. According to Lever, Spenser's attempt to break out of the courtly love convention with the Protestant-Platonist ideal of virtuous courtship was unsuccessful. "The true answer to the problem was found by Shakespeare. . . . What may be said with certainty is that, in taking the noble friend as his theme, Shakespeare freed himself from all the encumbrances which hampered the sonnet poets of his time" (276).

25. Joel Fineman, *Shakespeare's Perjured Eye: The Invention of Poetic Subjectivity in the Sonnets* (Berkeley and Los Angeles: University of California Press, 1986). Anne Ferry also considers Shakespeare's Sonnets crucial in the development of interiority, though Sidney figures as an important precedent (*The "Inward" Language: Sonnets of Wyatt, Sidney, Shakespeare, Donne* [Chicago: University of Chicago Press, 1983], 169).

26. Fineman, *Shakespeare's Perjured Eye,* 47.

27. Dowden, *Shakspere: A Critical Study of His Mind and Art,* 125–26. Dowden's study has the distinction of having run through more impressions than any other work on Shakespeare (thirty since 1875). For the exceedingly complicated problem of dating *Hamlet,* see Stanley Wells and Gary Taylor, *William Shakespeare: A Textual Companion* (Oxford: Oxford University Press, 1987),

122–23, 137–38. Wells and Taylor retain the traditional 1600–1601 date while conceding that the evidence cannot locate it more precisely than the early seventeenth century; indeed, it may still be the desirability of having *Hamlet* play the chronologically pivotal role in the canon which affixes it to the year 1600 rather than any evidentiary criteria.

28. Patrick Cruttwell, *The Shakespearean Moment and Its Place in the Poetry of the Seventeenth Century* (New York: Columbia University Press, 1955), 1. For the most explicit discussion of Shakespeare's sonnets as a fin-de-siècle phenomenon, see ch. 1, pp. 1–40.

29. Jameson argues that any concept of the synchronic assumes some sense of the diachronic (*Marxism and Form: Twentieth-Century Dialectical Theories of Literature* [Princeton: Princeton University Press, 1971], 327–40).

30. Like *century*, *decade* was also a collective noun frequently used as a literary division, as in Henry Constable's *Diana, or the excellent conceitful Sonnets of H.C. devided into viii decades* (1592).

31. See note 1 above. I remain grateful to Stephen Greenblatt for bringing this remarkable book to my attention.

32. In the early years of the church, time was counted from both the Crucifixion and the Annunciation, in addition to from the Nativity. It is around the time of Bede that A.D. begins to appear in Anglo-Saxon documents and comes to serve as the framework for English chronicles and annals. See C. R. Cheney, *A Handbook of Dates for Students of English History* (London: Offices of the Royal Historical Society, 1978), 1–2, and Milo, *Trahir le temps*, 9.

33. Hill, " 'Till the Conversion of the Jews,' " 270–71.

34. William Robertson, *History of the Reign of the Emperor Charles the Fifth* (1769), quoted by Schwartz, *Century's End*, 5.

35. See *L'an mille* (Paris: Gallimard, 1947), a collection of essays translated and collected by Edmond Pognon, which begins, "Des qu'il est question de l'an mille, le public pense fin du monde. . . . Or il ne correspond nullement a la verite historique" (vii). See also Milo, *Trahir le temps*, chs. 3 and 4, pp. 63–100. Schwartz cites these historians and others on the myth of the millennium in *Century's End*, 6–8, though he maintains that a new group of late-twentieth-century historians "are finding proof that apocalypticism *was* rife during the late 10th century" (31); his own thesis that since that "event" there has always been anxiety at the ends of centuries assumes such proof.

36. Jules Michelet, *Histoire de France* (1833–62; Paris, 1876), Vol. 2, ch. 4, pp. 88–89.

37. For a stunning recent act of self-periodization which draws on medieval trinitarian divisions, see Ruth Kestenberg-Gladstein, "The 'Third Reich,' " *Journal of the Warburg and Cortauld Institutes* 18 (1955), 245–95.

38. The great exception is Marx, who counters Hegel's idealized *Zeitgeist* with a system of periodization based on "a body of society" possessing historically contingent relations of production. See Balibar, "On the Basic Concepts of Historical Materialism," in Althusser and Balibar, *Reading Capital,* 253.

39. See the essays in Teich and Porter, *Fin de Siècle and Its Legacy,* all of which argue for some form of constructive change at the end of the nineteenth century.

40. See Gilles Deleuze and Felix Guattari, *Anti-Oedipus: Capitalism and Schizophrenia,* trans. Robert Hurley, Mark Seem, and Helen R. Lane (Minneapolis: University of Minnesota Press, 1983), and its application by Jameson, *Postmodernism,* 26–34.

41. Michel Foucault, *The Archaeology of Knowledge,* trans. A. M. Sheridan Smith (New York: Pantheon Books, 1972), esp. 3–17.

42. Quoted from an 1886 French article by Schwartz, *Century's End,* 159.

43. Erwin Panofsky singles out both Shakespeare's period for its obsession with time and Shakespeare for having repeatedly "implored, challenged, berated, and conquered Time" in his chapter "Father Time," in *Studies in Iconology: Humanistic Themes in the Art of the Renaissance* (New York: Harper Torchbooks, 1967), 92.

44. *John Donne,* ed. John Carey (Oxford: Oxford University Press, 1990), Meditation 17, 344.

45. For example, the date of Shakespeare's baptism is recorded in the Stratford parish register, April 26, but it is not until 1773 that the date of his birth is fixed at April 23, not coincidentally, St. George's Day. See Samuel Schoenbaum, *William Shakespeare: A Documentary Life* (New York: Oxford University Press, 1975), 20–24.

46. J. G. A. Pocock, *The Ancient Constitution and the Feudal Law: A Study of English Historical Thought in the Seventeenth Century* (Cambridge: Cambridge University Press, 1957), 54.

47. Patricia Fulmerton, following the memoirs of Sir Thomas Herbert (groom to the king during his captivity), relates that Charles I on his way to execution took along his personal silver clock, asked Herbert "the hour of the day," and then gave him the clock, bidding him to "keep it in memory of him" (*Cultural Aesthetics: Renaissance Literature and the Practice of Social Ornament* [Chicago: University of Chicago Press, 1991], 4–5).

48. See Thomas P. Roche, Jr., "The Calendrical Structure of Petrarch's *Canzoniere,*" *Studies in Philology* 71 (1974), 152–72, and its amplification in ch. 1 of *Petrarch and the English Sonnet Sequences,* 1–69. For a more expansive treatment of Petrarch's deictic and ritualistic temporality in the context of the Western lyrical tradition, see the first chapter of Roland Greene's *Post-*

Petrarchism: Origins and Innovations of the Western Lyric Sequence (Princeton: Princeton University Press, 1991), "Founding Fiction: The Temporality of Petrarch's *Canzoniere,*" 22–62.

49. "For the authors of many sequences of love sonnets mannered their eroticism with a cool deliberation, arranging individual sonnets—themselves often ardently passionate yet highly structured—in intricate symmetrical patterns or according to relatively recherché number symbolisms" (Alastair Fowler, *Triumphal Forms: Structural Patterns in Elizabethan Poetry* [Cambridge: Cambridge University Press, 1970], 174).

50. *Amoretti and Epithalamion,* ed. Alexander Dunlop, in *The Yale Edition of the Shorter Poems of Edmund Spenser,* ed. William A. Oram et al. (New Haven: Yale University Press, 1989).

51. For the numerological intricacies of the poem, see A. Kent Hieatt, *Short Time's Endless Monument: The Symbolism of the Numbers in Edmund Spenser's 'Epithalamion'* (New York: Columbia University Press, 1960); for more details and an overwhelming integration of them all, see Charlotte Thompson, "Love in an Orderly Universe: A Unification of Spenser's 'Amoretti,' 'Anacreontics,' and 'Epithalamion,'" *Viator* 16 (1985), 277–335.

52. See Roche, *Petrarch and the English Sonnet Sequences,* 430–35.

53. For another discussion of leaves and loss, see Gabriel Josipovici's discussion of the return of Hector's body to Troy in the *Iliad* ("Even as are the generations of leaves, such are those also of men") in "The Bible in Focus," *Journal for the Study of the Old Testament* 48 (1990), 101–22.

54. In his book of hours, the duc de Berry has himself portrayed in the illumination for January at a crowded feast in a hall dominated by a huge fireplace in front of which stands a chamberlain welcoming guests with the golden words "Approche, Approche." See *The Tres Riches Heures of Jean, Duke of Berry,* intro. and legends by Jean Lognon and Raymond Cazelles, trans. Victoria Benedict (New York: Braziller, 1969).

55. Representative of the intense scholarly attention paid in the 1940s and 1950s to the periodization of the Renaissance in history and art history respectively are Wallace K. Ferguson, *The Renaissance in Historical Thought: Five Centuries of Interpretation* (Boston: Houghton Mifflin, 1948), and Erwin Panofsky, *Renaissance and Renascences in Western Art,* 2d ed. (1965; London: Paladin, 1970), esp. chs. 1 and 2. For an account of the simultaneous Lovejoy-Wellek debate over romanticism and its more recent theoretical reverberations, see Mark Parker, "Measure and Countermeasure: The Lovejoy-Wellek Debate and Romantic Periodization," in *Theoretical Issues in Literary History,* ed. David Perkins (Cambridge: Harvard University Press, 1991), 227–47.

56. See Jameson's criticism of synchronic homologies and morphologies for

their "inability to project diachrony or to operate successfully in anything but a single instant or vertical cross section of time . . . in such a model, we are tempted to say, time can never run anywhere but down" (*Marxism and Form,* 325).

57. See Althusser's rearticulation of the Marxist conception of "social totality" in terms of a "structure in dominance" which consists of various semiautonomous levels running at different rates, developing unevenly and yet producing a totality, in Althusser and Balibar, *Reading Capital,* 91–105. See also Jameson's reflections on his own totalizing tendencies in "a time of nominalism" in *Postmodernism,* 399–413.

58. On the difficulty of extricating postcolonial studies from the imperialist ideology implicit even in the designation *postcolonial,* see Ella Shohat, "Notes on the 'Post-Colonial,' " *Social Text* 30/31 (Spring 1992), 99–113. On the necessity of excluding postcolonialism from the legitimating narratives of modernism still lingering in postmodernism, see Kwame Anthony Appiah, "Is the Post- in Postmodernism the Post- in Postcolonial?" *Critical Inquiry* 17 (Winter 1991), 336–57.

59. See Foucault's critique of "totalizing history" or "history proper," which "draws all phenomena around a single center," as opposed to "a general history" or "history improper," which replaces continuities with ruptures, origin with dispersion, in *Archaeology of Knowledge,* 10. See also his proposals for a Nietzschean counterhistory in "Nietzsche, Genealogy, History," in *Language, Countermemory, Practices,* ed. and trans. Donald Bouchard (Ithaca, N.Y.: Cornell University Press, 1977), 139–64.

60. Jameson, "The Vanishing Mediator," 2:10.

1690s

Unturning the Century:
The Missing Decade of the 1690s

Leo Braudy

MY TITLE is, of course, a play on the frequently quoted final line from Dryden's poem "A Song for St. Cecilia's Day, 1687," with its vision of the Last Judgment and the end of earthly history when "MU- SICK *shall untune the sky.*" The day consecrated to Saint Cecilia, the inventor of the organ, celebrated the necessary harmony of the religious, political, and aesthetic spheres. As Dryden writes in the poem, through the *"pow'r of sacred Lays"* God the Poet had created a divine harmony that brought all creation into being, and, in the last hour, the same music will destroy the material world of heaven and earth to create a higher harmony, beyond human understanding and expressible only in paradox.[1]

It may have been almost the last moment when such a faith could have been held without some self-consciousness about its implications. In the same year, Newton's *Principia Mathematica,* with its mathematical explanation of universal order, was published; within another year, William had landed at Torbay accompanied by a small army, a printing press, and, a few months later, John Locke.[2] James II, in the words of the parliamentary lawyers, then "vacated" the throne, and the Glorious Revolution was well on its way—a complex process that would include the appointment of Dryden's old adversary Thomas Shadwell as poet laureate as well as Thomas Rymer as historiographer royal when Dryden, originally offered the position, was disqualified after he refused to take an oath of allegiance to the new sovereigns.

In 1697, ten years after the first St. Cecilia's Day poem, Dryden writes another, called "Alexander's Feast," whose theme is not the overarching harmony of God's order for the heavens and the earth but the ability of the poet Timotheus, "the Mighty Master," to control both the emotions and the reputation of his erstwhile master, the grand conqueror Alexander. Dryden's assertion that artists are more important than monarchs has had a long cultural life. But 1697 also politically marks the acceptance by Louis XIV of William's rule over England and thereby the expanded parliamentary authority in matters of state it implied. What has been called the "War of the English Succession" (which began with the Long Parliament of 1641) was over, the accommodation between monarchic prerogative and parliamentary privilege was moving decisively into the parliamentary column, and the new model nation-state—to be imitated and extended in the French and American Revolutions of the next century—was in the process of being defined.

In the history of apocalyptic and millennialist thought, the 1690s across Europe mark the first time the last decade of a century was so generally perceived as a significant signpost of time, when the skies might very well be "untuned."[3] Historically, the political situation of the 1690s in England—a dual monarchy with Mary replacing William administratively while he is off at war against Louis XIV, an increased and increasing role for Parliament in executive decision making, an articulation of the "natural rights" of English citizens—also brings to a boil a conflict of ideas about the basic nature of England as country, society, nation, state, culture which have had long-lasting repercussions in Europe, the yet-to-be-born United States, and the rest of the world. As decades go, however, especially final decades of a century, the 1690s haven't gotten much of a good press. In the ranks of concluding decades, the 1590s, the 1790s, and the 1890s stand out much more vividly; in most literary histories, the 1690s seem not to exist at all. On either side, the Restoration and the Augustan Age bloat forward, the period from 1688 to 1702 squeezed between them.[4]

The canonized writers and anthologized works of the 1690s are few.

A handful of Dryden poems and the collaborations with Purcell get some recognition. Congreve, the one major author of the old canon who wrote in the decade, generally gets assigned to the Restoration, along with Vanbrugh and Farquhar, while Cibber becomes a footnote to Pope. Pope's pastorals, which are rooted in the quarrels of the decade, are declared to be proto-Augustan, and the fact that the author of *Tale of a Tub* tells us that he wrote in the year 1697 is ignored. Feminist criticism has begun to give Mary Astell's writings their due role in the gender realignment that was part of the period. But otherwise the quarrels that animated the 1690s have a musty, graduate-student air. There is some mention of the Phalaris controversy, which produced *Tale of a Tub;* of the Collier controversy over the morality of theater, which evoked responses from Congreve and Vanbrugh; of the Dispensary controversy over the relative professional rights of physicians and apothecaries, which inspired Samuel Garth to produce a poem celebrated in its day but now remembered primarily as the forerunner to *Rape of the Lock.* These, along with such other flotsam and jetsam as the pastoral controversy, the ancients and the moderns controversy, and the controversy over wit, are squeezed into asides or footnotes to the reading of a few poems.

Sometimes I think that this period has been scanted because no one has figured out an effective adjective for William and Mary. Certainly no one since Macauley has tried to make a case for its coherence (not that the Restoration and the Augustan period are such unproblematic wholes, although they appear that way for the purposes of most literary histories). Yet, through all these controversies flow similar winds of change, and, Swift in *Tale of a Tub* to the contrary, the empty windbags of Aeolus are found on both sides, as are the more fertile breezes.

Without scanting its parts or its contradictions, I think it is possible to see the British 1690s as both a complex and an incredibly decisive decade, a period of tremendous ferment, in which an impressive number of social and cultural myths first crystallized, whose long sway, only now, three hundred years later, at the end of another century, seems ripe for revision and certainly for reconsideration.

In a sense, the 1690s mark a national identity crisis, presided over by William and Mary, in which England begins to pass from a monocular nationalism defined by a single class interest to a binocular or multiocular nationalism in which various classes as well as individuals awaken to their own active stake in the definition of the country. A characteristic of the generation of the 1690s is to see human nature as a determining presence within society and culture, and to see society and culture as generated from human nature. The 1690s witnessed the birth of a nationalist consciousness distinct and often separable from the interests of monarchy and royalism, even among royalists themselves. They also saw the coalescence of a more abstract view of what constitutes England even among Lockean Whigs, for whom ownership of property was the necessary qualification for citizenship.[5] In France, the other European pioneer in centralized monarchy, the real state and the real estate were both identifiable with the monarch. In England, both questions—what is the real state and who owns the real estate—decisively became political issues. Parliament had been established both as part of the constitution and as one of the central elements in a new polity that was replacing the arena of the court. Instead of being assumed, the "innate" rights of Englishmen and the obligations of the monarchy were being spelled out.[6] Some final decades seem to be all summary, but the 1690s are the subtext of the next century—an era to be unpacked—not yet free of the past but looking toward a future, not so much a millennium or an apocalypse as the tabula rasa of time.

It is difficult to designate one central question in this, since I want to point to a constellation of changes that may not all necessarily have a single center. But if I were to choose an overarching issue, it would be the question of cultural authority (and I intend "culture" here to refer to everything that goes on in a society, not just its artistic productions).

Where is cultural authority to be found and who has it? A hundred years earlier it would have been easy enough to answer that question. Under Elizabeth, as well as James and Charles I, it is the monarch. During the Commonwealth, it is only Cromwell's resistance that prevents the urge of so many for a single principle and individual embodiment of authority from crowning him as well. With the Restoration, Charles II's right to the throne is assumed to be his inheritance, while royalist theorists and mythographers such as Dryden argue that it is his by his talent and experience as much as by his right: "Recov'ring hardly what he lost before,/His right indears it much, his purchase more" (*Astraea Redux,* 85–86). Thirty-four years later, during the reign of William and Mary, Dryden addressed Sir Godfrey Kneller, the "principal painter" to William III and thereby holder of an office, like poet laureate, valued by the Stuarts as part of their own royal propaganda. Yet in this poem Dryden hardly veils his belief that William entirely lacks the cultural authority that Charles II had before so comfortably embodied.

In France at the same time, Colbert and Perrault were elaborating Richelieu's assertion of a centralized culture whose program was that all artistic production, all cultural activity, had as its prime goal the enhancement of the glory of the monarch. But in the England of William and Mary, the exclusive cultural centrality of the monarch— under attack since the Commonwealth period, reaffirmed during the Restoration, allowed to slip away by James II—was being totally redefined. Dryden, of course, sees this not as a redefinition but as an absence, a loss. As he says to Kneller, "Thou hadst thy *Charles* a while, and so had I./But pass we that unpleasing Image by." Why is that loss of true patronage acceptable? The next lines give the reason. "Rich in thy self; and of thy self Divine,/All Pilgrims come and offer at thy Shrine" ("To Sir Godfrey Kneller," 100–3). Here, as Dryden does so often in his poems of the 1690s, he reaches out not only to other poets and playwrights but to painters and musicians as well, to affirm the central cultural role of the person he often calls the "godlike" artist. As a result of the Glorious Revolution, the indefeasible right of hereditary inheritance may have been lost to the monarchy, but in the history of art and literature, if Dryden has his way (and to a great extent he did), aesthetic inheritance and continuity will stand supreme.[7]

From the 1660s to the 1680s Dryden had been the most effective formulator and propagandist for the view that monarchy and hierarchy are "natural." In the 1690s he helps lay the groundwork for the secular celebration of the poet as a cultural power more in touch with the basic rhythms of national value than any politician or religious leader—and the history of art, all the arts, as more stable and continuous than that of politics or institutional religion. As if to emphasize how literature stands beyond politics, Dryden in the preface to the *Fables* (1700) cites Milton as one of his great forebears, "for we [writers] have our Lineal Descents and Clans, as well as other Families."[8]

Although Dryden's poetic/artistic replacement for the monarch is still constructed upon the monarchic model, it has an interesting post-monarchic twist. In "To my Honour'd Kinsman, John Driden, of Chesterton in the County of Huntingdon, Esquire," included in the *Fables,* he plays on the coincidence of names to make an analogy between the poet and the good politician:

> Two of a House, few Ages can afford;
> One to perform, another to record.
> Praise-worthy Actions are by thee embrac'd;
> And 'tis my Praise, to make thy Praises last.
>
> (203–6)

In his kinsman John Driden, as in himself, the private virtues traditionally praised in royalist pastoral are identified with the supposed neutrality and political virtue of what is in fact the anti-William country party:

> A Patriot, both the King and Country serves;
> Prerogative, and Privilege preserves:
> Of Each, our Laws the certain Limit show;
> One must not ebb, nor t'other overflow;
>
> . . . .
>
> When both are full, they feed our bless'd Abode;
> Like those, that water'd once, the Paradise of God.
>
> (171–74, 178–79)

It is easy enough for us (although not for Dryden) to see in retrospect how the decoupling of the authority of art from that of religion and politics potentially licenses all sorts of literary outsiders and opposers to claim the same sanction, and in their turn to claim a greater cultural centrality and importance for authority in the poem than for authority in the state. In this unorganized but clearly outlined movement to define English culture separately from that of the ruling court and class, elements of what might be called the beginning of cultural relativism are apparent, a movement away from official sanctions to the sanction of new groups and new individuals. Again, the figures of William and Mary seem crucial to the change. A Dutch court and an Anglo-Dutch monarchy in the 1690s have a far greater impact on the definition of Englishness than had the advent of James I from Scotland almost one hundred years before. In great part this is due to William and Mary's own reticence about imposing themselves as monarchs, unlike the divine-right Stuarts. Once again the contrast with France is sharp. Louis XIV's view of monarchy embraced the idea that the country was his personal property, whereas the view of government which William had landed to enforce was more akin to Locke's belief that all property belonged to individuals as a basic right, along with life and liberty. In only one of many examples, Charles II in the last years of his reign and James in the beginning of his had continued the so-called quo warranto proceedings, which removed the charters of towns and corporations until they could be reaffirmed by the monarch as being solely in his gift and not sanctioned by some alternate urban succession. When William came to the throne, those cases were reversed by act of Parliament and the abrogated charters restored, including that of the Massachusetts Bay Colony.[9]

William and his supporters, of course, made many gestures toward the kind of centralizing monarchic imagery which so animated the Stuarts, but he was much more immediately concerned to create a financial and political system that would support his wars against Louis XIV than with imitating Louis's grandeur and *gloire*. When William's head is substituted for Cromwell's on an engraving, it should be remembered that in a similar engraving forty years before, Cromwell's had been substituted for that of Charles I. The realization that emblems can be detached from one association and adventitiously linked to an opposing political position is an essential insight that is a by-product of the visual and poetic polemics of the Restoration. In a manner intriguingly like our own experience in the twentieth century, a larger and larger public had learned to decipher visual meaning and by that deciphering take an ironic stance toward the mechanics of its creation. With the 1690s, such readable imagery is domesticated into personal gardens (a favorite of William and Mary) rather than being a mainstay of public propaganda, and the object with truly new visual impact is the increasingly popular mezzotint, with its delicate ability to create a shaded, rounded, and dimensional picture of an individual. The mythic imagery of English monarchy had been worn out both by repetition and by association with arbitrary power, and it was rapidly being replaced by the tangible structures of what one historian has called the "more effective central administration of William III," in which power was diffused through a bureaucracy of state and quasi-state institutions.[10]

In a sense, William's durability in the period (Mary was much more generally liked) owed more to the many different opinions that were voiced about him, pro and con, than to any unitary identification with Alexander or Aeneas or Hercules floated by some of his artistic flatterers.[11] As Defoe was to say in "The True-Born Englishman" in 1700, speaking as "Britannia":

> No parallel from Hebrew stories take,
> Of godlike kings my similes to make:
> No borrowed names conceal my living theme;
> But names and things directly I proclaim.
>
> . . . .
>
> He needs no character but his own fame,
> Nor any flattering titles, but his name.
> William's the name that's spoke by ev'ry tongue:
> William's the darling subject of my song.
>
> . . . .
>
> For fame of families is all a cheat,
> 'Tis personal virtue only makes us great.
>
> (921–24; 929–32; 1215–16)

Marvell saw Cromwell as David, and Dryden followed suit but cast Charles II in the role. Defoe's version of William III as Everyman would be for Dryden equivalent to no sanction at all.[12]

Stressing efforts such as Dryden's to replace the political and religious centrality of the monarch with the aesthetic singularity of the poet diverts attention from another hallmark of the 1690s, the expansion of a free, or at least freer, press and the encouragement of many voices. The univocal monarchic practice of legally requiring government pronouncements to be read in every church service lapsed into virtual disuse, as part of what William Speck calls a "partial disestablishment of the Church of England during the reign of William and Mary."[13] As one loud voice was stilled or at least muffled, many others were brought into being. William, as I mentioned, arrived in England complete with printing press, and one of the first acts of the London populace after the Convention Parliament invited him to assume the throne (December 11) was to attack and destroy the exclusively licensed presses of James II's printer Henry Hills, a recent Catholic convert. A flood of book people of all sorts—writers, makers, publishers, many in self- or government-imposed exile since the 1680s—returned home. By 1694, Parliament had refused to extend the Licensing Act, not so much because of a principled belief in a free press, but because no faction—Whigs, Tories, Jacobites, Commonwealthmen, nonjurors, Williamites, atheists, deists, or defenders of Anglican orthodoxy—could muster enough votes to silence the others. In effect, the underground polemics, which had been available only to the daring as part of the extensive clandestine circulation of books and manuscripts during the Restoration, now joined the aboveground cultural mix. In a familiar example, a good portion of the polemical poetry stretching back to the 1660s began to be printed in a virtually official set of volumes called *Poems on Affairs of State.* Precensorship was eliminated, and blasphemy, treason, or other malfeasances were to be punished ex post facto by common law. Public opinion, if not yet quite born, was certainly well beyond the embryonic phase. Parliament's new status within the constitution, along with the mandating of more frequent elections, brought with it the possibility of public argument and difference of opinion. The figure of Defoe, celebrated by the public although put in the stocks by the government, is a compelling indication that even common-law prosecution was neither a preemptive nor an irrefutable response to the power of opinion.[14]

The presaging polemic of many of these changes, Locke's *Two Treatises of Government* (published in 1689, although written earlier), hardly repudiates monarchy. Its preface explicitly states that the works were written to support the claim of William, "our Great Restorer," to the throne. But the central project of the *Two Treatises* is to displace the patriarchal justification of monarchy with a theory of contract and consent. In no way is the monarch a special person exempt from ordinary human nature, nor does he have inherent rights, other than those confirmed in the contract between monarch and people.

It is through this contractual view of political relations that Locke undermines both the patriarchal and the paternal metaphors for royal authority. Most of the *First Treatise* attacks Sir Robert Filmer's *Patriarcha: A Defense of the Natural Power of Kings against the Unnatural Liberty of the People* with its legal derivation of royal authority from an inheritance that goes back to Adam. Why, asks Locke, is Filmer's view of biblical authority so exclusively male? Where is Eve in all this? Where is the mother? Even though woman in general may be cursed, any individual woman can still avoid damnation, and simply because Adam was created first, he has no more inherent right to power than Eve. Particularly in creating, raising, and educating the child, women have an equivalent and perhaps an even greater right. Neither the relation of biblical patriarch to his descendant, nor that of the father to his child, provides an appropriate model for our relation to the state. It is analogous instead to the relation between husband and wife, equal contracting partners.[15]

I am not arguing that Locke is a feminist, and no one could claim that Locke's collective writings are entirely free of patriarchal biases. William III, after all, was the legal administrative power in England, because he had refused a tory offer that Mary rule and he be regent. Nevertheless the shift in emphasis from father to husband, from inheritance to contracting parties, should be underlined. It certainly was by the Jacobite attacks on William and Mary in the poetry of the period, in which the most common analogy was to the story of Tullia, who instigated the murder of her father by her husband and then drove her chariot over her father's body on the way home.[16] Like Mr. Harlowe writing to Clarissa some fifty years later, James II even warned his daughter in a letter that if she accepted the crown, she would feel "the curse of an angry father . . . as well as of a God who commanded obedience to parents." When she died, he forbad mourning in his court.[17]

The argument of Locke's *Second Treatise* is thus that it is contract and consent that create the political state. In certain moods, public opinion may consider the nation on the model of a family relation (and this has been a tory and conservative trope down to the present). But Locke's nation-state is also a reasonable and readable structure that needs logical justification and institutions less dependent on class and family alignment than on reason and policy. Part of the intriguing amalgam engendered by the reign of William and Mary was the cultivation of both aspects: the nuclear family as a model and staging area for society; the nation-state as an affective structure that engendered feeling for *itself* much more than for anyone who happened to be at its head. With the Act of Settlement in 1701, Parliament decisively assumed the power of determining, with a nod to genealogy, who the monarch should be. The desacralization of monarchy which began with the execution of Charles I was virtually complete, and Anne, Mary's sister, became the last monarch either to veto an act of Parliament or to appear among her people to cure them with her touch.

A decisive aspect of this affective nationalism being shaped in the 1690s was the class-conscious assertion of an as yet virtually inarticulate middle class against the perceived aristocratic hegemony of the Stuart court. Literary history, for instance, has judged harshly what has been called the sentimental drama of the 1690s (exemplified in the plays of Cibber and to a lesser extent in those of Vanbrugh and Farquhar), in contrast with the full-blooded comedies of Etherege, Wycherley, Dryden, and Congreve (while conveniently forgetting that Congreve himself worked entirely in this period). Critics have tended either to focus on seemingly neutral formal questions of genre or to indict "bourgeois morality" as the suffocator of Restoration exuberance and energy.[18] But just as William drew upon new financial networks and political sanctions to prosecute his wars, so under the sponsorship of Mary morality became a political issue in what D. W. R. Bahlmann called "the moral revolution of 1688." Mary took the lead in encouraging justices of the peace to prosecute vice and the clergy to preach moral reform perhaps more than conformity to the Church of England. Shortly after he assumed the throne, William for his part wrote to the Bishop of London: "We most earnestly desire and shall endeavor a general reformation of manners of all our subjects as being that which must establish our throne and secure to our people their religion, happiness, and peace, all of which seems to be in great danger at this time by reason of that overflowing of vice which is too notorious in this as well as other neighboring nations."[19]

Although the societies for the reforming of vice take up more of the public space, both the rigidity and the relativity of moral standards were issues of the 1690s. Locke's arguments against innate ideas, for example, tended to undermine any absolute moral standards. As Frederick Copleston paraphrases Locke, "If moral principles were really innate, we should not find those differences in moral outlook and practice in different societies and different epochs which we do in fact find."[20] Natural tendencies, argued Locke, were not the same as innate principles, and so moral precepts could be justified socially and even naturally, but not absolutely.

But this preoccupation with manners and corruption is also tinged with the resurgence of a providential world-view that owed something to the coming end of the century with its millennialist need to be pure for the Apocalypse. Only one of the many manifestations of the moralizing part of the current was Jeremy Collier's 1698 attack, *A Short View of the Immorality and Profaneness of the English Stage,* which prompted retorts from Congreve, Vanbrugh, Dennis, and others, followed by almost innumerable defenses and responses by Collier himself. This so-called Collier controversy indicates clearly how much the desire for a moral theater is a class-conscious attack against the Stuart monarchy and its court more than an aesthetic position devoid of history or context. Even Collier, a nonjuror who refused to swear allegiance to William, could still champion the William and Mary program of establishing the authority of the monarchy and thereby the government in moral rather than genealogical terms. In December 1697 after the Peace of Ryswick ended his wars with Louis XIV (for the time being) and established his legitimacy, William reemphasized the central place of morality in his political program in an address to the House of Commons: "I esteem it one of the greatest Advantages of the Peace that I shall now have Leisure . . . effectually to discourage Profaneness and Immorality."[21]

Yet no matter how critics such as Rymer tried to reassert theatrical decorum and the unities as an analogy to a morally and socially coherent society, theater in the 1690s, through its own evolution and through the changing cultural world it inhabited, was losing forever its formerly direct relation to the royalist cosmology. Even as it attempted to reject its aristocratic and courtly lineage thematically, theater as a cultural space still seemed unable to express the new nationalism. Morality had become a party or at least a factional issue, and no matter who had managed to capture it, the immediate losers were the Stuarts and those perceived as their aesthetic fellow travelers. Dryden in 1692, at the end of a eulogy for a woman he never met ("Eleonora"), writes that he "dares to sing thy Praises, in a Clime/Where Vice triumphs, and Vertue is a Crime" (363–64). But the conceit, although no doubt sanctioned by satiric tradition, has a somewhat defensive sound. As the most prominent artistic Carolingian extant, Dryden was to bear a good deal of the brunt of the literary attacks against Restoration court culture and on wit itself which grew during the decade, especially those of the self-important poet-physician Sir Richard Blackmore, who appears as the leader of the moderns in Swift's *Battle of the Books*. Blackmore's ideal, embodied more persuasively by Defoe, is a plain-speaking and thereby truly English style: "How happy were the old unpolished Times,/As free from Wit as other modern Crimes?" (13–14). Wit is not only immoral and repellent in itself; it also enervates the energies needed for national destiny: "Their minds for Empire form'd would never quit/Their noble Roughness, and dissolve in Wit./For Business born and bred to Martial Toil,/They rais'd the Glory of *Britannia's* Isle" (20–23).[22]

Much of literary criticism in the 1690s is thus an argument about society and culture posed as an argument about theater and literature, whether the polemicist is Dryden, Rymer, Dennis, Bentley, Blackmore, Collier, or Congreve. It deals with issues that decades later were still treated as if fresh by Addison, Steele, Pope, and Swift. In essence, the question for Scriblerians and non-Scriblerians alike is the same: Who is the audience for art, and can that audience be trusted? What must be said and what can be left unsaid? All have somewhat different ideas about this, mixing moral, political, and aesthetic assumptions. Those, like Collier, who are uncertain about the audience's ability to understand, want to co-opt art for explicitly didactic purposes. Those, like Defoe or Swift, who wish to divide the good audience from the bad audience, experiment with irony. Those, like Addison and Steele, who wish to enlighten the good audience and educate the ignorant audience, encourage detachment and taste, in the manner of *The Spectator.*

The government of William and Mary sought to have morality on its side even more definitely than religion, while implying that morality was in some way a larger category than any institutional religion. In this increasingly personalized and individualized politics, sexuality was the crossroads of nature and culture. William and Mary asserted in essence that their political legitimacy was due to the greater morality of their court than Charles II's; and it is no coincidence that such an assertion should originate in a dual monarchy of husband and wife. Wit, said Blackmore, was a noxious alloy that needed purification just as William had recoined the currency. Changing the metaphor, Swift, imitating the modern perspective in *Tale of a Tub,* remarks on "that large portion of wit laid out in raising pruriences and protuberances."[23] In combat with these images of sexual impurity was the marriage of William and Mary.

"At once a lover and a king," says Defoe in praise of William's relation to Mary in "The True-Born Englishman" (936), and the determination both of gender distinctions and of the proper definition of each gender's nature constitutes another intriguing element of the decade. Both between and within the genders, the polemics of Blackmore, Collier, and others against the Restoration thinly veil an attack upon Restoration male sexuality: its libertinism, its homoeroticism, its masculine self-display, and its foppery; and on Restoration female sexuality, its promiscuity, its avidity, and its behind-the-scenes court power. Mary Astell's *Serious Proposal to the Ladies* (1694), for instance, faces masculine brutality and destruction of female identity in marriage with a proposal that women with a personal destiny larger than marriage can retreat to a monastic setting or (in a later edition) to an academic college. Congreve's *Way of the World* (1700) somewhat differently marks the change from sex as a prime subject of comedy in 1660s to money in 1690s, underlining the repercussions of Locke's contract theory in the personal as well as the public realm. Mirabell, nominally the rake, demonstrates his good nature by financially looking out for Millamant, while Marwood and Fainall, the devious manipulators, are left out of the resolution. In the proviso scene, Mirabell and Millamant (with their oddly cross-dressed names) negotiate the complexities of their willingness and unwillingness to be married, by exploring in some detail a contract theory of male-female relations that assumes that heterosexual monogamy—the intersection of male legal power and female sexual power—needs legal language to make it work.[24]

The reign of William and Mary thus introduces to English politics and thereby to English culture the explicit idea that heterosexual monogamy is the norm, that other forms of sexuality are the deviation, and that the upper classes are the unnatural garden of such deviations, unless proven otherwise. A grim prospect for the future, we might say. But nothing in cultural change cuts only one way, and, if we can clear away some of our aesthetic prejudices, we can also see how the sentimental drama of the period, both comedy and tragedy, is more preoccupied with psychological issues—how people connect beyond and beneath social forms—than are all but a few plays of the Restoration. Humour characters disappear, and even fools have their reasons. Whereas so much of previous drama was set in public spaces, now more private worlds are dramatized. The failures and difficulties of sexuality begin to take up more dramatic space than do the sprees. As the standard of sociability and connection becomes more enveloping, the issue of solitude arises, a necessary precondition for both the experience and subject matter of the novel.[25]

I have been characterizing the 1690s as an important, even decisive, moment in the separation of aesthetic and moral sanctions from religious and political ones, a moment that insensibly engenders the rise of a secular state in which culture, rather than monarchy and religion, supplies the greatest portion of nationalist affect. Instead of a pyramidal structure with the monarch at its head, as in the familiar frontispiece to Hobbes' *Leviathan,* England in the 1690s moves toward a definition of the nation as connective tissue, a web of relations between institutions rather than an institutional hierarchy. What had been the central and defining cultural icon of the monarch is being displaced by a variety of other models and possibilities. Defoe's mockery of the need for a biblical typology to justify William was evidence of a ferment over how to typify the nation and the interconnections of its major institutions. It was followed in the reign of Anne by such works of political satire as Bernard Mandeville's *Fable of the Bees* (first version, 1712), which characterized England as an enormous hive, and Sir John Arbuthnot's *History of John Bull* (1714), in which its political and economic travails are presented through the domestic drama of a family headed by a clothier, whose name, like that of Uncle Sam, would later become the synonym for the entire country.[26]

A crucial step in this development was the changing nature of the economy and the changing character of money and the erosive effect it would have on the concept of inherent hierarchical social rank as well as on the nature of individual self-definition. The 1690s mark the consolidation of capitalist finance in England, more specifically, its enabling paraphernalia (credit, banks, debt, insurance, limited liability), some elements of which had appeared earlier but which only now arrived as a package. It was this financial engine that would drive the Industrial Revolution, as well as English expansionist imperialism in the eighteenth century. The immediate structural reason for the creation of the national debt in 1693 and the founding of the Bank of England in 1694 was the need to fund William's wars and give the lie to the expectation of both Louis XIV and James II that England would be defeated because it would go broke. But one intriguing effect was that more and more people had a financial interest in the government, by lending money to it. In 1672, Charles II could deal with his overwhelming debts by merely declaring a Stop of the Exchequer and defaulting. But even though the financial crisis of 1696 may have been just as bad or worse, by then the monarch was contractually obligated to lenders who came from a greater variety of classes and backgrounds than before.[27] The engagement with government activities became more intense, and therefore the need of the government to justify its policies to a larger and larger audience became a more pressing issue. At the same time, war itself was becoming less an opportunity for an aristocratic class to gain personal honor than a means, sometimes for those same aristocrats or their sons, to oppose a tyrannical enemy of the nation (e.g., Louis XIV) and to expand the nation's economic interests, whatever they thought of that nation's current monarch.[28]

The connection forged by William and his finance ministers between war, money, and public opinion instituted more efficient ways for the monarch to get the money he needed, but it still seemed in line with the past urges of the Stuarts to do the same thing. What significantly marks the 1690s, however, is the growing appreciation for the abstract possibilities of money—the translation of material riches held tangibly in the present into wealth, whose power extends into the future through credit, speculation, long-term debt—and, not least, confidence. The entrepreneurial imagination could be protected from disaster by insurance, as well as the pooling of resources for projects in limited liability companies; and the flow of wealth could be more easily and flexibly tapped by the new assignability and negotiability of bills of exchange.[29]

Against ideologies in which stability was virtue and the future either a pit of darkness or an ascent to heaven, the financial innovations of the 1690s emphasized the positive qualities of change and the arena of earthly value. As we can see three hundred years later, none of these changes have been unmixed blessings, and most have had both deeply negative as well as positive effects on human society. But rather than condemn them for what they have become, I would like instead to see them in the context of the period in which they were instituted. Swift's impersonation of his own worst nightmares of himself as a hack writer totally bound to the present in *A Tale of a Tub* dramatizes the ambivalence and confusion of writers caught between the old world of static order and the new world of Locke and Hobbes, in which "restlessness" itself is a salient human characteristic. But Pope, for one, never quite realizes to what extent his own status as an out-of-political-power moral force was itself licensed by the personal leverage he usually satirized and mocked as "paper credit."

The strange wrestlings that Swift, Defoe, and Pope have with their public images and the vexed authority of writer and work parallel the shifting values of the 1690s. Convinced that monarchical authority is now groundless, Dryden moves to assume its aura on his own public credit. Swift and Defoe are much more uncertain, despite the one's disdain for and the other's fascination with the new world of money. The funding of the national debt and the founding of the Bank of England mean in effect that money, not the land or power or personal prestige of any particular dynasty, has become the foundation and continuity of the state's continued existence. The creation of the national debt assumed that loans would be repaid no matter who ruled, and England would still exist, independent of the provident or improvident monarch.

Money conceived as wealth and linked to a sense of time that differed from the linked aristocratic and gentry values of genealogy and land is another step toward a nationalism separable from the beliefs of a particular monarch and class—and, I would argue, it indicates a growing sense of class division and cultural relativism in the period. Another pervasively abstract way of relating phenomena was through the speculations of physical science, whereby Newton, for example, could merge a deductive extraction of general principles with an inductive emphasis on experimentation. What is particularly intriguing about the cultural place of science in the 1690s is the gradual acceptance of the idea that scientific knowledge could be independent of both religious and political coloration. Like Locke's empiricism, which rejected indwelling substances (such as the soul) that defined all creation, as well as innate ideas inside human beings, Newton's view of the orderly interconnections in the physical universe rested on the principles of mathematics and the observations of the scientist. The organization of matter is a crucial part of the properties and effectiveness of the universe. But that organization is distinguishable from what is organized, and therefore there is no need to postulate an external sovereign principle. Locke particularly emphasized the impress of environment onto character as an argument against the need for postulating a soul.[30] In another implication, teased out further by later philosophers of the body like La Mettrie, there was therefore no need to postulate a soul in order to understand human identity.

Both Locke and Newton did hold on to God as the last remnant of a belief in a sovereign principle in nature, like that of Hobbes in politics. But their idea of God, as their deistic followers, if not they themselves, were eager to assert, was not a necessary principle in their theories. It needed no validation by any particular religious institution and was therefore primarily personal.[31] Both, in other words, were interested in giving an account not of stasis but of change, Newton by trying to create an unchanging mathematical system of relationships, Locke by considering questions of individual development.

In their emphasis upon experience as the major source of knowledge and their effort to fashion that experience into general principles, both Newton and Locke raise central questions of perception and epistemology: How do we know things? And what is it we know? Locke particularly highlights the developmental in understanding, and it is tempting to relate his sense of how knowledge grows in the individual to his position as tutor of Shaftesbury's grandson virtually from the moment of the boy's birth (1671). Just as in his labor theory of value the mixing of sweat and soil created property, so in his theory of knowledge the observer created meaning from experience through perspective. We can understand the world not only through direct experience but also by contemplating our own understanding of it, and thereby progressively correct what we think and do.

Such ideas are intriguingly reflected in the many literary controversies of the period over the nature of interpretation and what credentials the interpreter ought to have. Here, perhaps for the last time so ferociously and exclusively, battles about politics and culture are fought out primarily through literary means. In these arguments, the literarily canonized writers and their associates tend to be on the side of sensibility rather than on the side of evidence. What many of these writers perceived politically was a society held together more and more by cash, competition, and contract—what tory propagandists called "money and multitude"—rather than the traditional relations on which their own prestige depended. Faced with a new and confusingly fragmented audience, and the loss of their own social and cultural space, these writers devised a term to bridge the gap between money and class. That term they called taste.

The Phalaris controversy particularly pitted the aristocratic defenders of sensibility (and therefore taste) against adversaries whose bond was that they believed in a primarily philological approach to classical texts and, hardly incidentally, were neither scions nor the associates of the old royalism. The seemingly trivial specific issue—the authenticity or the inauthenticity of the text of the fourth-century (A.D.) letters of Phalaris, a Sicilian ruler of the fifth century B.C.—indicates that, like much of the ink spilled over deconstruction by its critics and defenders, the Phalaris controversy involved energies and passions more sweeping than the strictly literary. The real fight was instead over who gave authoritative readings and interpretations. One side in the Phalaris controversy, the side of Temple and Swift, essentially argued that the epistles were well written, said true things, and were therefore authentic. The other side, the side of Richard Bentley and supporters such as Blackmore and even Locke, argued that if the text was not historically authentic, it made little difference what it said or how well it was written. Hardly anyone seemed to notice (or perhaps they repressed) that, in these letters, Phalaris is exonerating himself from the charge of cruelty for roasting the sculptor Perillus in the brazen bull the sculptor himself has constructed. No wonder perhaps that the defenders of the greater wisdom of the ancients should fight their battle in support of a classical tyrant, while the moderns should attempt to disarm the text of its authenticity and power. The story of Phalaris is an object lesson of the relation between patrons and artists—a myth for the 1690s, as the story of Daedalus and Minos, with the allegiances appropriately reversed, would become an enabling myth for James Joyce in the 1890s.

In scholarly terms Bentley is in fact right, and he becomes one of the great figures in classical studies. But the position of Swift—with its hostility to science, to analysis, to academics from the wrong classes, and explicitly to criticism itself—is the one that has come down to us as the true aesthetic counterblast to the nitpicking philologists. Preserved as if in amber by the Scriblerians, it animates a good deal of Augustan satire, and its emblematic figures still preoccupy Pope almost forty years later in *Dunciad IV.* I am not here trying to document the beginning of the two cultures, as R. F. Jones formulated the ancients and moderns argument many years ago. But it useful to remember that sometimes pedantic and self-important fools can be smart and right, whereas visionary and self-important great writers can be petty and blind about what is truly significant in their own times.

With the separation of the realm of absolute truth (religion) from that of relative truth (politics), the aesthetic becomes a new kind of absolute on earth. But, instead of being irrevocably tied to a specific class and background, taste develops into a capacity of the self potentially possessible by anyone willing to learn. As the third earl of Shaftesbury, Locke's young student, later argued, both "good taste" and "good sense" could be coaxed out through learning, and it was not necessary to believe in God in order to be moral and have good taste (although he hoped religious belief, morality, and good taste would usually correspond).

On taste depended the effort to create a psychic connection to otherwise lost English greatness that would correct and reform the new monied classes. Taste was the morality by which, according to such propagandists as Pope and Addison, both aristocrats and bankers could find absolution. Thus taste became the conceptual means of retooling elite attitudes for a postmonarchic world, a crucial element in the democratization of art and artists. Its deployment enabled what I have elsewhere called "aristocrats without ancestors" to make their claims on public attention, so that someone like Pope—a Catholic who couldn't vote, hold public offices, or otherwise be considered an English citizen—might yet aspire to and become the central cultural figure of a generation. Thus begins the familiar pattern of the opposition between the alienated artist and the co-opted politician, along with an association between social marginality and moral centrality that helped create a new audience for art.

Literary and aesthetic history thus begins its tangled relation to political and economic history with the crisis in the 1690s over the way the individual connects with the state, religion, and the universe and what elements in each sphere contribute to personal identity. In this crisis, Locke's distinction between society and state seems crucial. As Locke argued, society was superior to the state because the state could always be changed if society still remained, whereas if society were lost, the state would go with it.[32]

When we contemplate the last decades of centuries, let alone millennia, the 1690s for me stand out for their fertility and ambiguity, more in the root meaning of *apocalypse,* the lifting of a veil, than in the drumbeating macho apocalypses we are used to invoking, on the model of the revolutionary decade of the French 1790s. I've been trying to sketch the different languages of the 1690s, with some suggestion of how they may connect without fitting too neatly. I haven't stressed the echoes of our own time, because I think they're both clear and yet uncertain enough in their implications to lay too heavy an interpretive burden upon them. But if the question of the 1690s is "who am I and what is England?" our own similarity is apparent.

In the attempt to disentangle the politics and culture of this period, two elements stand out: (1) the difficulty of consistently aligning all of anyone's opinions or any group of opinions as part of one or another "party"; and (2) the difficulty of understanding the causes of a cultural action from its later effects, or of defining the effect by a knowledge of the causes—what Edward Hall has called "the essential indeterminacy of culture."[33] J. A. Downie has remarked that "like so many of the consequences of the Revolution of 1688, the freedom of the press came about by accident rather than design." Similar things could be said about the later influence of Locke's theory of government, Newton's theory of gravitation, and Dryden's praise of the "godlike" artist. Perhaps in a time of fertility and ferment, that's the point.[34]

One final question, to use the language of millennialism, is whether the 1690s expected a deliverance to come from Time, or *in* Time. Newton calculated that the Beast would fall in 1867 and the millennium commence in the year 2000, and Donald Wilcox has recently argued that only after Newton did people refer to living in their centuries.[35] In other words, a century was beginning to be seen as containing and influencing the events inside it, rather than the group of events collectively determining the century. Certainly Dryden seemed to think something like this was happening—and he didn't particularly like it. The attitude embodied in his writing is summarized wonderfully in one of his last works, "A Secular Masque," whose Horatian title punningly invokes the age itself as well as the new secularity of meaning. Janus, the god of beginnings and endings, calls on a weary Chronos to hurry toward the century's end, while Momus, whom Swift associates with the goddess Criticism, mocks both of their efforts. Stung, Janus calls successively on Diana, Mars, and Venus to praise what they have accomplished in the last one hundred years. They try, while Momus and Chronos point out that neither the virgin goddess of the hunt and nature, nor the manly god of war, nor the goddess of love, can muster any lasting accomplishment:

	All, all, of a piece throughout;
[To Diana]	Thy Chase had a Beast in View;
[To Mars]	Thy Wars brought Nothing about;
[To Venus]	Thy Lovers were all untrue.
	'Tis well an Old Age is out,
	And time to begin a New.

By the time "The Secular Masque" was published in 1700, Dryden was already dead.

NOTES

1. The celebration, which was instituted in England in 1683 after Charles II's triumph over the Shaftesbury forces in Parliament, eagerly invites a propagandistic reading. Dryden's poetry before 1696 is quoted from *The Works of*

John Dryden, vols. 3–4, ed. H. T. Swedenberg, Jr., et al. (Berkeley and Los Angeles: University of California Press, 1969, 1974). After 1696, it is quoted from *The Poems of John Dryden,* vol. 4, ed. James Kinsley (Oxford: Oxford University Press, 1958). Line numbers appear parenthetically in the text.

2. William landed on November 5, 1688, the anniversary of Guy Fawkes Day, a celebration frequently devoted to anti-Catholic festivities, as well as the day after both his thirty-eighth birthday and the anniversary of his marriage to Mary (1677). Locke arrived with Princess Anne on February 12, 1689.

3. Utopian and millenarian expectations hardly need a final decade of the century to get going, but its imminence surely adds fuel. In seventeenth-century England, millenarian expectations had been excited and then dashed by the coming of the years 1656, the year of the Flood, and 1666, the year of the Beast. See Christopher Hill, " 'Til the Conversion of the Jews," *Millenarianism and Messianism in English Literature and Thought, 1650–1800,* ed. Richard H. Popkin (Leiden: Brill, 1988), 16–56. In his very erudite volume *Century's End: A Cultural History of the Fin de Siècle from the 990s through the 1990s* (New York: Doubleday, 1990), Hillel Schwartz concludes therefore that "the 1690s had been practically eviscerated of dramatic potential by events earlier in the century" (114) and that it was "a decade neither spectacular nor tragic nor frightening nor mysterious" (121).

In contrast, see G. S. Rousseau, "Mysticism and Millenarianism: 'Immortal Dr. Cheyne,' " in *Millenarianism and Messianism:* "The 1690s was understandably the great decade of chiliasm and millenarianism in Western Europe" (87). Rousseau also cites chiliastic interpretations of the Treaty of Ryswick (1697) that concluded the millennium was at hand (88). Millenarian writers also interpreted William's escape from an assassination plot in 1696 as further evidence that the new Constantine, one of the prerequisites for the millennium, was present on earth. See John Whittel, *Constantinus Redivivus; or, A Full Account of the Wonderful Providences, and Unparallel'd Successes that have all along attended the Glorious Enterprises of the Heroical Prince, William the 3d . . .* (London, 1693); and *A Short Review of the Remarkable Providences: attending our Gracious Sovereign William the IIId, 1693 to the present* (London, 1699).

Milleniannism: or, Christ's Thousand Years Reign Upon Earth Considered. In a Familiar Letter to a Friend (1693) argues the orthodox Anglican view that millenarianism is a Jewish heresy that mistakes Christ's reign for an earthly kingdom. Handwritten notes in both the Clark and the Union Theological Seminary libraries copies ascribe *Milleniannism* to Lancelot Addison, Joseph's father, who had also written books on Islam and Judaism. But Donald Wing in his *Short-Title Catalogue* (1945) calls it anonymous. It is not cited in the *Dictionary of National Biography;* nor is it included in the collected edition of *Dean Addison's Works.*

4. With even broader assertion, G. M. Trevelyan's *Social History of England* (1942), for example, goes immediately from Restoration England to "The England of Defoe," while the Restoration chapter itself ends somewhat prematurely with a description of the Great Fire of 1666. The corresponding sections in his earlier *History of England* (1928) are filled almost exclusively with William III's wars.

5. That is, the ability to vote and be elected to office. Many of the next generation of Augustans believed this as well; and yet Hume with his *History of England* (1754–62) helped create through book ownership a good part of the basis for a non-landowning nationalistic popular culture, as in their own ways had Addison with his *Spectator* papers on *Paradise Lost* and old English ballads, Gay with *The Beggar's Opera,* Fielding with such songs as "The Roast Beef of Old England" (in *The Grub-Street Opera*)—to cite only a few examples. Although folks songs and broadsides about national issues had existed for some time, the Glorious Revolution may also mark an important moment in their popular influence. "Lillibulero," one of the most familiar and long lived, is frequently credited with a widespread influence on army morale. See, for example, Claude M. Simpson, *The British Broadside Ballad and Its Music.* New Brunswick, N.J.: Rutgers University Press, 1966), 449–55.

6. It has recently been argued by John Pocock and other historians and political scientists that the Declaration of Rights and other documents of the Glorious Revolution really didn't say anything that hadn't been said or implied before. But they ignore the rhetorical and cultural importance of what might be called articulating the innate. For another view, see Lois G. Schwoerer, "The Bill of Rights: Epitome of the Revolution of 1688–1689," in *Three British Revolutions: 1641, 1688, 1776,* ed. J. G. A. Pocock (Princeton: Princeton University Press, 1980), 224–43. Kenneth H. D. Haley concludes that "the main political effect of the Revolution was to transform Parliament from an event into an institution" ("International Affairs," in *The Age of William III and Mary II: Power, Politics, and Patronage, 1688–1702,* ed. Robert P. Maccubbin and Martha Hamilton-Phillips [Williamsburg, Va.: College of William and Mary, 1989], 49).

7. Dryden's attitude toward the relation of artist and patron seems heavily indebted to the model of the Italian Renaissance. William Aglionby translated eleven lives from Vasari as part of *Painting Illustrated in Three Dialogues* (1685), whose preface includes a passing reference to "our late Blessed Monarch," with whom "all *Arts* seemed to return from their Exile." Dryden's translation of Du Fresnoy's *De Arte Graphica* appears in 1695. (The second edition in 1716 marks the first publication of Pope's "To Jervas.")

The appointment of Shadwell, whom Dryden had attacked almost fifteen years before as "MacFlecknoe," to replace Dryden as laureate has naturally evoked remarks such as that of James Anderson Winn's about "the devaluation of the post of Poet Laureate" ("*The Laureateship,*" in Maccubbin and Hamilton-Phillips, *William III and Mary II,* 322). But the possibility remains that decentering the Stuart emphasis on the arts was part of William and Mary's program; furthermore, the post of laureate was a political post, not an aesthetic one, and Dryden himself had done his best to define it that way.

8. Kinsley, *Poems,* 1445. The growing popularity of Milton as a great writer rather than condemnation of him as a political sectarian is illustrated by the several editions of *Paradise Lost* in the 1690s. There is none between the third edition of 1678 and the fourth of 1688. Then comes a fifth in 1691, with a reissue the next year, a sixth in 1695 with notes by Patrick Hume, and three volumes of prose, prefaced by a life by John Toland, in 1698. Other praise includes that of the young Joseph Addison in "An Account of the Greatest English Poets" (1694). Dryden, of course, had already produced *The State of Innocence,* his "tagged" version of *Paradise Lost,* in 1677. His epigram comparing Milton to Homer and Vergil prefaced the 1688 edition of *Paradise Lost.*

9. Blackstone's brief but authoritative commentary on the quo warranto cases can be found in William Blackstone, *Commentaries on the Laws of England,* ed. Joseph Chitty (London, 1826), 1:485. The fullest historical and legal account is by Jennifer Levin, *The Charter Controversy in the City of London, 1660–1688, and Its Consequences* (London: Athlone Press, 1969). See also D. W. Jones, "London Merchants and the Crisis of the 1690s," in *Crisis and Order in English Towns, 1500–1700: Essays in Urban History,*" ed. Peter Clark and Paul Slack (London: Routledge, 1972). Gerald E. Frug gives a useful overview of the basic issues in "The City as a Legal Concept," *Harvard Law Review 93* (April 1980), 1057–1154.

10. William A. Speck, "Religion, Politics, and Society in England," in Maccubbin and Hamilton-Phillips, *William III and Mary II,* 64.

11. As William J. Cameron writes, "Even the Jacobites' obsession with the Usurper helped to make William III an omnipresent figure" (*Poems on Affairs of State: Augustan Satirical Verse, 1660–1714,* vol. 5 [New Haven: Yale University Press, 1971], xxv).

12. "The True-Born Englishman," in *Poems on Affairs of State: Augustan Satirical Verse, 1660–1714,* vol. 6, ed. Frank H. Ellis (New Haven: Yale University Press, 1970), 260–309. The choice of Hercules, Aeneas, and Alexander as iconographic twins to William is nevertheless intriguing, since each had a hero-as-one-of-us side that could be used to undermine the idea of sacred monarchy. Another intriguing contention over issues of cultural nationalism is the undeclared battle over who owned Arthur. Dryden and Purcell's opera

King Arthur appears in 1691. On the problems Dryden had in revising for the reign of William III what in origin had been for Charles II, see Curtis Alexander Price, *Henry Purcell and the London Stage* (Cambridge: Cambridge University Press, 1984). The importance of the character of Merlin reflects the "godlike" artists of Dryden's poetry of the 1690s. In contrast, Richard Blackmore's *Prince Arthur* (1695) celebrates William III in the person of Arthur and incidentally parodies Dryden as Laurus. His own *King Arthur* appears in 1697.

13. Speck, "Religion, Politics, and Society," 53. A crucial event was the petition of the Seven Bishops against being required to order local priests to read James II's Declaration of Indulgence—one of the precipitating acts of the Glorious Revolution. See David Ogg, *England in the Reigns of James II and William III* (Oxford: Clarendon, 1955), 166–67, 198. Although five of the seven bishops later refused to swear allegiance to William III and William frequently ordered royal proclamations to be read during services, the traditional connection between church and state embodied in such concepts as the divine right of kings, passive obedience, and nonresistance had been decisively undermined. See Ogg and also C. R. Cragg, *From Puritanism to the Age of Reason: A Study of the Changes in Religious Thought within the Church of England, 1660–1700* (Cambridge: Cambridge University Press, 1950).

14. Between the passing of the Triennial Act in 1694 (which enforced parliamentary elections at least every three years) and the Septennial Act in 1715 (which put the period back to every seven years), there were more elections than ever before, or since. David Ogg notes that this habituation to a regular rhythm of dissolving and summoning parliaments had an influence on the evolution of party politics (*James II and William III*, 492).

15. It has been argued that Locke began writing at least the *First Treatise* years before as a response to Filmer, who died in 1653. According to James Daly in *Sir Robert Filmer and English Political Thought* (Toronto: University of Toronto Press, 1979), *Patriarcha* was written in 1635–42. But it was republished in 1680 during the Popish Plot crisis, and Locke specifically ties his comments to that edition because, as he says, it has been explicitly drawn upon by "the Pulpit" and is "the Currant Divinity of the Times" (156), making Filmer "the great Champion of Absolute Power, and the idol of those who worship it" (159–60). *Two Treatises of Government* was published anonymously, and Locke never publicly acknowledged authorship, but he listed the book as one of his anonymous works when willing it to the Bodleian. See the discussion in Peter Laslett, ed., *John Locke: Two Treatises of Government* (Cambridge: Cambridge University Press, 1960), 45–66.

On patriarchalism, see Gordon J. Schochet, *Patriarchalism in Political Thought: The Authoritarian Family and Political Speculations and Attitudes, Especially in*

Seventeenth-Century England (New York: Basic Books, 1975). Susan Moller Okin in *Women in Western Political Thought* (Princeton: Princeton University Press, 1979) argues that "Locke in fact uses the mother's 'equal title' as a *reductio ad absurdum* to refute the derivation of political from parental authority" (200). See also Carole Pateman, *The Disorder of Women: Democracy, Feminism, and Political Theory* (Stanford: Stanford University Press, 1989), and Diana H. Coole, *Women in Political Theory: From Ancient Misogyny to Contemporary Feminism* (Brighton, England: Wheatsheaf, 1988).

16. According to the *Oxford Classical Dictionary,* Tullia first got her brother-in-law to murder her husband so that she could marry him.

17. Howard Nenner, "The Rule of Monarchical Succession," in Maccubbin and Hamilton-Phillips, *William III and Mary II,* 22, quoting Sir John Dalrymple, *Memoirs of Great Britain and Ireland,* 1771–73, app. pt. 2, 15. See also Hester W. Chapman, *Mary II, Queen of England* (Westport, Conn.: Greenwood, 1976 [a reprint of the 1953 Jonathan Cape edition]). The letter is not mentioned in Elizabeth Hamilton, *William's Mary: A Biography of Mary II* (New York: Taplinger, 1972).

18. Robert Markley in *Two-Edg'd Weapons: Style and Ideology in the Comedies of Etherege, Wycherley, and Congreve* (Oxford: Clarendon, 1988) has recently proposed a more refined model for the interaction of personal psychology, generic compulsions, and cultural context. The modern critical uneasiness with sentiment intriguingly reflects the growing disdain at the time for the expression of emotion in both religion and social life that was cultivated by many in the upper classes, as well as imitators like Swift, who was said never to have laughed or hardly even smiled in his whole life.

19. William's letter is dated February 13, 1689. It asks the clergy to read laws against blasphemy, swearing and cursing, perjury, drunkenness, profanation of the Lord's day, and the like whenever they preach sermons against such vices. William, according to D. W. R. Bahlmann, was more nervous about the religious societies encouraging moral reform, since they were so often made up of working-class dissenters. The Church of England in fact opposed most of the reformation societies. See Bahlmann, *The Moral Revolution of 1688* (New Haven: Yale University Press, 1957), and also Shelley Burtt, *Virtue Transformed: Political Argument in England, 1688–1740* (Cambridge: Cambridge University Press, 1992).

20. Frederick Copleston, *A History of Philosophy,* vol. 5 (Garden City, N.Y.: Doubleday, 1964), 84.

21. Quoted by Ellis, *Poems on Affairs of State,* vol. 6, 130, from the *Journals of the House of Commons,* vol. 12, 1.

22. *Poems on Affairs of State,* vol. 6, 135.

23. *A Tale of a Tub and Other Works,* ed. Angus Ross and David Woolley (Oxford: Oxford University Press, 1986), 274; see also 319.

24. Compare also the treatment of divorce and marriage in Farquhar's *Beaux' Strategem* (1707). Princess (later Queen) Anne was very taken with Astell's project and pledged financial support until Gilbert Burnet persuaded her otherwise.

25. Rousseau writes to D'Alembert much later in the century that the essential characteristics of the English are a taste for fiction and for solitude. In *Robinson Crusoe,* for example, the entire class system seems extractable from the solitary self.

26. M. Dorothy George in *English Political Caricatures* (Oxford: Clarendon, 1959), 1:11, notes that there is a "considerable time-lag" between Arbuthnot's use of the figure of John Bull in *Law is a Bottomless Pit* and his appearance as a cartoon figure no earlier, it seems, than 1756. Unlike David Low, who revived John Bull in World War II, Arbuthnot's view was almost entirely negative.

27. Both Locke and Newton were much involved with issues of money in the 1690s, usually on the side of hard currency. Newton was made Warden of the Mint in 1695 and Master in 1699. Locke was similarly opposed to paper credit, although his philosophy of knowledge in some ways supports it by implication. For Locke's writings on money, see Patrick Hyde Kelly, ed., *Locke on Money,* 2 vols. (Oxford: Clarendon, 1991), especially the very thorough introduction.

28. Aristocracy's exclusive relation to war was being undermined, and matters of honor were becoming a concern of the state as much as of the aristocratic individual, looking forward, for example, to the eighteenth-century stigmatizing of dueling.

29. See P. G. M. Dickson, *The Financial Revolution in England: A Study in the Development of Public Credit, 1688–1756* (New York: St. Martin's, 1967), 3–89; and Sir John Clapham, *A Concise Economic History of Britain from the Earliest Times to 1750* (Cambridge: Cambridge University Press, 1963), 262–305, and *The Bank of England: A History* (Cambridge: Cambridge University Press, 1945), 1:1–52. In volume 6 of William S. Holdsworth's *History of English Law* (London: Methuen, 1903–72), chapter 7 ("The Latter Half of the Seventeenth Century") deals with changes in financial and business law. See also J. R. Jones, *Country and Court: England, 1658–1714* (Cambridge: Cambridge University Press, 1978), ch. 3 ("Administration and Finance"). Recently, some of this analysis has been attacked by John Brewer, *The Sinews of Power: War, Money, and the English State, 1688–1783* (New York: Knopf, 1989).

30. In contrast, Hobbes' attack against the idea of the soul derives from his substitution of the state for religion as the prime organizer of sociability.

31. Newton notably refused to comment on whether gravity was a structure inherent in matter or placed there by God. He might identify gravity in some moods with a kind of providence, constantly emanated by God, but the identification had little to do with whether his theory worked. Like Milton, he seemed to believe in a God like that in *Paradise Lost*, Book 10, who sends his angels out to create the imperfectly working universe from the symmetrical universe before the Fall. John Toland, in contrast, called gravity a vital force unconnected with God. Toland followed Giordano Bruno's formulation that the only true religion is worship of nature itself.

32. Locke's opposition between state and society is an early consideration of the relation between base and superstructure, and one in which superstructure wins.

33. Edward Hall, *The Hidden Dimension* (Garden City, N.Y.: Doubleday, 1966), 102. For a similar perspective in the terminology of the period, see Hume, "On the Rise and Progress of the Arts and Sciences," in *Essays Moral and Political* (Edinburgh, 1742).

34. J. A. Downie, "Politics and the English Press," in Maccubbin and Hamilton-Phillips, *William III and Mary II,* 343. So often "unanticipated results" occur because the assumptions of a previous age are still being made. What unanticipated results will come from our own faulty assertions, as well as our hidden assumptions, we'll have to wait and see.

35. Donald Wilcox, *The Measures of Time Past: Pre-Newtonian Chronologies and the Rhetoric of Relative Time* (Chicago: University of Chicago Press, 1987). Newton's calculations are in *Observations upon the Prophecies of Daniel, and the Apocalypse of St. John* (London, 1733). See Schwartz, *Century's End,* 126. The word *century*, if not the precise meaning, is popularized by *Les vrais centuries et propheties de Maistre Michel Nostradamus* (1558), in which it refers to the one hundred stanzas of each book of prophecies. Although, as Schwartz notes, Nostradamus was particularly attracted to "ends of centuries and ends of millennia" (*Century's End,* 100), the French language still prefers *siècle* to *centurie* to denote both age and century, as in Charles Perrault's celebratory poem "Le siècle de Louis le Grand" (1687).

1790s

The Literal World of the English Della Cruscans

Jerome McGann

There are few fallacies more common than the opinion that poetry should mimic the daily speech.
Ezra Pound, "I Gather the Limbs of Osiris"

IN ENGLAND as well as France, the last decade of the eighteenth century is associated with revolutionary upheaval and the promise of energetic change. We don't now tend to think of the century as having a "decadence" at all. But decadence—in the (proper) late-nineteenth-century understanding of the term—did come to the late eighteenth century, only it came retrospectively. Reading the scene through the cultural program founded by Wordsworth and Coleridge, later buttressed by the tradition of Arnold, scholarship was able to define a literary decadence that ran from approximately 1760 to 1795. On one end stood the Ossianic fragments, on the other the climactic decadence of the Della Cruscan movement. In between fell an evolving body of "graveyard" verse and other highly mannered styles of poetic "sensibility."

From a late-eighteenth-century perspective, however, this tradition of sentimental poetry was not at all seen as "decadent." On the contrary, even its latest Della Cruscan flowering was perceived in a very different way. When sworn enemies of the Della Cruscans such as William Gifford and T. J. Mathias denounced such writing, they did so because it seemed to them—to appropriate a pair of other later terms— too radical and avant-garde both in its style and in its politics. The project launched in 1798 by Wordsworth and Coleridge was a consciously designed alternative to recent sensational trends in poetry, and particularly to the innovative movement that had taken 1790s England by storm: the poetry of the Della Cruscans. Only later, when the Wordsworth/Coleridge perspective became culturally normative, would it seem possible to judge the Della Cruscans as "decadent." The notable stylistic features of their work—extreme artifice of expression, erotic subject matter, and a theatrical self-consciousness—would be turned from gestures of innovation and originality to "marks of weakness, marks of woe."

The "decadence" of the Della Cruscans, therefore, conceals a large and important problem in literary history as well as the relation of literary history to the formation of literary judgments. These problems center in the status of so-called sentimental poetry, for which the Della Cruscan movement was the most important, the most coherent, and the most influential exponent. Every one of the so-called major romantics was deeply marked by sentimental conventions of writing, and there is an important (unremembered) sense in which Keats, Shelley, and Byron are the supreme legacy of the Della Cruscan movement in particular. As we know, during the past 150 years or so the terms *bad* and *sentimental* have grown virtually synonymous so far as poetry is concerned. But sentimental poetry is neither good nor bad; it is a certain kind of writing which evolved out of a particular (eighteenth-century) set of ideas.

Literary history has by now more or less accepted this view of the matter so far as fiction is concerned, but it has not thought to apply the same way of thinking to verse. As a result, it isn't too much to say that we have all but completely lost the ability to read sentimental poetry, because its stylistic codes have been largely erased from our (short-term) memories.

In this situation, the case of the Della Cruscans assumes a large cultural significance—too large for an essay of this kind. My immediate object is not to tackle the complex literary-historical issues but to make some preparation for such moves. I want simply to begin a process of reading a paradigm form of late-eighteenth-century sentimental verse. To attempt anything more at this point would be, in my view, premature.

À Rebours

I don't know anyone now who takes Della Cruscan writing seriously, and even its readers are rare. The received judgment—that it's trash— comes to us as naturally as the leaves to the tree. Nor do many now recall the immense notoriety the Della Cruscans quickly gained after their initial appearance in the 1780s. William Gifford, the movement's first public enemy, launched his (once celebrated) attack in 1791 be- cause Della Cruscan writing was so successful, becoming what Gifford called an "epidemic malady . . . spreading from fool to fool" (intro- duction to *The Baviad*, xii).[1] The disease ran out of control when Rob- ert Merry (alias "Della Crusca") returned home to England from Italy

> and immediately announced himself by a sonnet to Love. Anna Matilda [Mrs. Hannah Cowley] wrote an incomparable piece of nonsense in praise of it; and the two "great luminaries of the age," as Mr. Bell call[ed] them, fell desperately in love with each other. From that period not a day passed without an amatory epistle . . . and a thousand other nameless names caught the infection; and from one end of the kingdom to the other, all was nonsense and Della Crusca. (xii–xiii)

Gifford's terms of abuse are interesting: for example, "high flown," "prurient," "obscene," "unintelligible." Three good couplets in an im- possibly turgid satire summarize his views:

> Lo, DELLA CRUSCA! In his closet pent,
> He toils to give the crude conception vent.
> Abortive thoughts that right and wrong confound,
> Truth sacrificed to letters, sense to sound,
> False glare, incongruous images, combine;
> And noise, and nonsense, clatter through the line.
> (*The Baviad*, 39–44)

Leaving aside the indiscriminate abuse—can it really be the case that *all* this writing comes out as sh——t?—we will find, I think, that Gifford here betrays a good general comprehension of what this ("unintelligible") writing is about. His understanding is just marked with a negative inflection. The "incongruous images" are everywhere, elaborate sound patterns build primary stylistic devices, and knowledge (moral or otherwise) generally lies closer to a surface of textual "letters" than to a subsurface of deeper "Truth."

If we want to reacquire an understanding of Della Cruscan poetry, Gifford's fustian points us in the right direction, but it won't take us very far. We need a more serious antagonist for that. Fortunately we find what we want exactly at the end of the decadent and Della Cruscan nineties—in the poetry written by Wordsworth and sponsored in his "Preface" to the 1800 *Lyrical Ballads*. This great prose text is a conscious critique of the Della Cruscans and the kind of writing inspired by their work. When Wordsworth speaks of his subject as "incidents of common life," when he says he wants to trace "the primary laws of our nature" in a rural language of "simple and unelaborated expressions," and when he attacks "arbitrary and capricious habits of expression [that] furnish food for fickle tastes and fickle appetites of their own creation," he is setting his project apart from the manner of the Della Cruscans. The famous paragraph on "the general importance of the subject," in which Wordsworth attacks literary London's "degrading thirst after outrageous stimulation," is leveled squarely at the Della Cruscans, whose influence on the theater of the decade had earlier (1795) drawn Gifford to his second attack, in *The Maeviad*.[2]

Wordsworth's response proved effective for a simple but profound reason: unlike Gifford, he could write good verses, so he put into play a practical alternative to what was not a set of ideas, confused or otherwise, but a style and program for writing. Of course such conflicts of style always reflect broad social and cultural issues. The ideological stake for Wordsworth involves the relation of language to "feeling," both natural (so called) and poetic. Feeling is the central issue because the Della Cruscans had launched their own writing fifteen years earlier under the same sign. From Wordsworth's perspective, however, nothing could be more strained or artificial than the feelings pursued by writers like Robert Merry and Mrs. Cowley. And (so the imagination goes) when feelings are stimulated rather than spontaneous, when poetic language cultivates artifice rather than sincerity, Wordsworth's mind turns catastrophic, fantasizing a world reduced "to a state of almost savage torpor."

All such totems and taboos aside, clear lines are being drawn here that will have marked effects upon the course of writing and culture. Shelley's and Byron's hostilities with Wordsworth, for example, like Blake's earlier, come from their greater sympathy with a Della Cruscan approach to language. The differences come sharply into focus if we compare the way Wordsworth renders external nature with a typical Della Cruscan text. The first passage, a familiar one, comes out of Wordsworth's "Lines Written in Early Spring"; the second is from Robert Merry's "Monody Addressed to Mr. Tickell."

> To her fair works did nature link
>   The human soul that through me ran;
> And much it grieved my heart to think
>   What man has made of man.
>
> Through primrose tufts, in that sweet bower,
>   The periwinkle trail'd its wreathes;
> And 'tis my faith that every flower
>   Enjoys the air it breathes.
>
> The birds around me hopp'd and play'd:
>   Their thoughts I cannot measure,
> But the least motion which they made,
>   It seem'd a thrill of pleasure.
>
>   (5–16)

> Yes, *she was mild and lovely as the star*
> That in the Western hemisphere afar,
> Lifts its pure lamp above the mountain's head,
> To light *meek Evening to her dewy bed.*
> And as the waning moon displays,
> With mirror clear, Morn's rising rays,
> She, in decay, show'd VIRTUE'S ORB refin'd,
> Reflected *fairer* from her angel mind;

> Till at the last too fierce a blaze was given,
> *And then she sunk from sight, and* FADED *into* HEAVEN.
>
> (1:72)[3]

Both of these passages involve what a later criticism, unhappy with romantic conventions of writing in general, would call "affective fallacy"—the ascription of sensibility to the inanimate or vegetable world. The two texts represent, however, very different approaches to the natural world, human feelings, and the language of poetry.

Wordsworth's lines, a *locus classicus* of "romantic nature," call for little comment at this late hour. As everyone knows, the text illustrates how one might "see into the life of things" in the broad (religious and philosophical) sense Coleridge invoked when he spoke of "the one Life within us and abroad." Merry's natural scene at first appears shot with a similar kind of spiritual presence and activity. In fact, Merry is far from perceiving, much less arguing, that some kind of objective "soul" or transcendent spirit "runs through" the natural world.

> O TICKELL! in the murm'ring gale
> Oft have I found thy plaintive voice prevail;
> When the wet fingers of the morn
> Shook the cold pearl-drops from the bending thorn;
> Or when, at close of day,
> To the lone vale I took my way,
> The *sad vibration of faint* ECHO's *breath,*
> Brought to my heart the dirge of Death.
>
> (1:70–71)

Here the lively features of the natural world come forward as signs of a power Blake called "the Human Imagination." In this respect Merry's poem is unconcerned with nature as such—for example, whether or not it is invested with spirit. What interests him is art's capacity to deal with fatal circumstance. In trying to console Tickell, Merry celebrates what he elsewhere calls the "Eternal beauties in [the] mind" (1:12).

The natural figures conjured in Merry's poem are thus, paradoxically, signs of their opposite, signs of an antinature. Like so much of the late nineteenth century's aesthetic writing, Merry's poem doesn't simply construct an artificial order of nature; it puts its own act of construction on display, makes that act one of its primary concerns: winds and vibrations displace human sounds, morning turns statuesque, trees are bejeweled. The infamous extremities of Della Cruscan poetry are self-consciously theatrical and spectacular, like the self-conscious wit cultivated in (for example) metaphysical poetry. Here is Anna Matilda describing dawn in a landscape she imagines Della Crusca is traveling through:

> And when her tints of various dye
> Burst from the pallid sickly sky,
> *There* rush in violet, *there* in green,
> *Here* in soft red imbue the scene,
> Then lose themselves by growing bright,
> 'Till swallowed up in one vast flood of light—
>
> (1:103–4)

This is the metaphysical verse of a period that has put itself to school to sensationalist rather than faculty psychologies. Everything is as it is perceived. So while "nature" is constantly invoked in Della Cruscan verse—while the entire movement took the meridian graciousness of Italy as its point of departure—the Della Cruscans definitely operate under the Blakean proverb "Where Man is not Nature is barren."[4] The primary forms of nature dwell in "the feeling mind" (2:26):

> Why does thy stream of sweetest song,
> In many a wild maze wind along;
> Foam on the Mountain's murm'ring side;
> Or through the vocal coverts glide?
>
> (1:78)

Della Crusca's artful questions to Anna Matilda are asked in the "vocal coverts" of this text, which is constructed as a linguistic landscape—indeed, which is (implicitly) arguing that the primary forms of nature are inward, imaginative: human.

So when Della Crusca answers his own questions by saying these things happen "because thy HEART can feel," we register the difference between this order of feeling and (say) Wordsworth's. The "one Life" perceived and celebrated by Wordsworth and Coleridge is a religious vision, an imagination of the

workings of one mind, the features
Of the same face, blossoms upon one tree;
Characters of the great Apocalypse,
The types and symbols of Eternity
Of first, and last, and midst, and without end.
                    (*Prelude,* Book 4, 636–40)

While such a vision, like Della Crusca's, is ultimately grounded in eighteenth-century sentimentality, it also reaches for the sublime, an effect (or what we now call an "aura") which is explicitly refused in the sentimental tradition followed by Merry, Cowley, and their immediate precursor, Sterne.

Refining Decay

Wordsworth and Coleridge have embarked on a quest for permanence, for a "primal sympathy / Which having been must ever be." By contrast the Della Cruscans, for all their celebrated extremities, operate at a distinctly mortal level. Wordsworth's transcendental functions appear in Della Crusca as imaginative ornament and decorative wit. What we observe are not the workings of one transcendent mind but the artificial constructions of a particular poet—"one" mind in distinct lowercase. So whereas Wordsworth's poetry typically aspires to the spontaneous and sublime, Della Cruscan poetry, like later aesthetic poetry, seems self-conscious and erotic. These differences signal different approaches to poetic style and a desired mode of address toward the reader. Della Cruscan verse is conversational where Wordsworth's is meditative, theatrical rather than overheard. The Della Cruscans court passion and intensity, but in doing so they leave no doubt that these are all splendid and wonderful *im*permanences. The Della Cruscans thereby erect what Blake will call "the buildings of Los[s]"— extreme artifices of an eternity in love with the productions of time, and hence in a permanent condition of impermanence.

We see this approach very clearly in Merry's "Monody" for Tickell. Tickell's wife, Maria, has passed away like the moon before the dawning sun; "FADED *into* HEAVEN" is a pure grace of art, an imagining as fragile as it is lovely, and a splendid figure of the permanence of impermanence. As the rest of the poem makes quite clear, Merry writes— *sympathizes*—out of an understanding that *"all of Nature, as of Art, must end"* (1:72). The superb (and distinctly proto-Shelleyan) figure of Maria Tickell fading into heaven is not a transcendental but a quotidian sign. Working from the same Enlightenment traditions out of which Merry came, Shelley will name it a sign of "Intellectual Beauty." So will Coleridge, in "The Eolian Harp" (line 47). Although he was strongly influenced by the Della Cruscans in the early nineties, his ambivalence begins to emerge in "The Eolian Harp" (composed in 1795). His later, famous critiques of sensationalist philosophies, as we know, are as much recantations as anything else.[5]

The point is that while both Wordsworth and Merry wish to celebrate "the mind of man," that mind is for Wordsworth the type of a higher Mind, whereas for Merry it is always a particular mind. Wordsworth's "types and symbols of Eternity" are Merry's "Eternal beauties *in thy* mind" (my italics): "thy" signifying that the addressee, in this case Anna Matilda, comprehends such eternities, and "in" specifying the locus of what we might otherwise take for an appeal to a transcendental norm. Furthermore, Della Cruscan beauties are "Eternal" in a distinctly Lucretian or Heraclitean (rather than a Platonic or Neoplatonic) sense. In this respect the writing draws explicitly upon the materialist tradition of sentimentality defined by Sterne, the immediate (and acknowledged) precursor of the Della Cruscan movement.[6]

To the Della Cruscan imagination, one enters nature only to reconstruct its orders in a finer tone. The transformation doesn't occur, however, as an act of creation—a unique fiat—but as *re*creation, a multiplying of particular repetitions. Eros therefore defines this second-order creation, which emerges—in current terms—by fusion rather than fission energy. In this context, we can appreciate why the typical form of Della Cruscan writing came to be the *tenso,* and its defining event the poetic interchange of 1788–89 between Della Crusca (Robert Merry) and Anna Matilda (Mrs. Hannah Cowley).

The general form of these interchanges was well suited to their conflation of eros and artifice. Consciously following the example of the troubadours and the *stil novisti,* the English Della Cruscans refined the *tenso* into a specifically heterosexual erotic exchange. The *tensi* of their European precursors were more typically between male poets, whether friends or rivals or both. In English Della Cruscan verse, by contrast, what were once poetic subjects for male poets—their blessed damozels—assume positive textual roles, become themselves agents in the poetic exchanges. Furthermore, the focusing interchange (in this defining case between Della Crusca and Anna Matilda) generates further textual relations with third or fourth parties. For example, the first *tensi* of Della Crusca and Anna Matilda are complicated when two other figures ("Reuben" and "Laura") enter the central poetic conversation.

These kinds of development and complication are inevitable, however, given the erotic and dialectical character of the writing. Indeed, the Della Cruscan movement came into such rapid cultural dominance during the 1790s, I think, because the writing explicitly encouraged further writing, whether response or elaboration. Its erotic formalities appealed as much to women's as to men's imaginations. Such a catholic (hetero)sexuality elsewhere provoked the hostile reactions best known through Gifford's *Baviad* and *Maeviad* and the other attacks of the period, such as Polwhele's *Unsex'd Females.* Conventional literary history now likes to imagine that those attacks undid the English Della Cruscan movement, but the truth is that it pursued a vigorous life well into the 1830s. Byron and Keats are both deeply marked by Della Cruscan forms, and the resources of the style are not fully exploited until it is undertaken by Moore and Shelley.[7]

Nonetheless, its basic poetic structure is clearly visible from the start. We may trace its unwindings, for instance, in the central passage of Della Crusca's early lines "To Anna Matilda" (1:86–88):

> Let but thy lyre impatient seize,
> Departing Twilight's filmy breeze,
> That winds th' enchanting chords among,
> *In ling'ring labyrinth of song:*
> Anon, the amorous *Bird of Woe,*
> Shall steal the tones that quivering flow,
> And with them soothe the sighing woods,
> And with them charm the slumb'ring floods;
> Till, all exhausted by the lay,
> He hang in silence on the spray,
> Drop to his idol flow'r beneath,
> And, 'midst her blushes, cease to breathe.
>
> (1:87)

Anna Matilda's poetry is being imagined here as a kind of aeolian harp whose chords "seize" an otherwise inarticulate natural world and compel it to a form of complex, world-creating music. The verse thus produces a landscape of intoxicating sound out of which appear music-generated supernatural forms: in this case, a watered woodland covert where the eternal loves of the rose and the nightingale are replayed.[8] The verse is profoundly synaesthetic and transformational. It is a "labyrinth of song" where lyre and breeze wind into each other, where *flowers* alternately *flow* like water or turn to sculpture (idle idols), and where the nightingale's erotic suspension quivers like (or into) a drop of dew that is falling into (its) love and, in that ecstatic moment of morning, dying.

Della Crusca ascribes such events to the power of Anna Matilda's poetry, but of course this magical world appears only in the here and now of Della Crusca's poem. Nonetheless, the relations of rose and nightingale, of lyre and breeze, and of the various other interchanges evoked by the verse are all *figurae* of the defining interchange, the poetic *tenso* between Della Crusca and Anna Matilda. The basic structure of the verse is exactly erotic because it proceeds by acts of intercourse which are at once perfectly immediate and purely imaginative.

"Sex in the head" then; but after all—so the Della Cruscans, like Blake, will ask—where else *should* it be? In our vegetable nature? An injunction to cultivate a sensate mind involves here the imaginative reconstruction of Blake's vast polypus of death, our (erstwhile and otherwise) brute flesh. As Blake was fashioning that reconstruction in cosmic and world-historical terms, the Della Cruscans—like Oscar Wilde one hundred years later—rediscovered it in the pulsation of very ordinary arteries.

The miniatures of Della Crusca, the movement's apparently precious trifles and triflings, mark a self-conscious effort at a comic recovery of energy. Gifford and others were appalled that the Della Cruscans' fame should have emerged through such lowbrow periodical organs as the *Oracle* and the *World*. But the movement gloried in its scorn for "those the VULGAR call the GREAT" who "strive a consequence to find / By seeming more than Human kind" (1:79). "Consequence" follows rather when "the lustre of poetic ray / [Shall] wake an artificial day" (1:11): "artificial" here standing as the sign of an imagi-

William Blake. Watercolor illustration for Edward Young's Night Thoughts. *Night Two, verso of title page. 1796. British Museum, London.*

nation that aspires to be at once supremely self-conscious and wholly voluptuous.

The eighteenth-century term for that ideal was Intellectual Beauty. Though commonly understood to involve mental as opposed to sensuous phenomena, Intellectual Beauty defines a project to undermine the body/soul distinction altogether. When Merry opens his exchange with Mrs. Cowley by publishing his intention to quit poetry, she writes to dissuade him:

> O! seize again thy golden quill,
> And with its point my bosom thrill;
>
> (1:3)

The self-consciousness of such eroticism—it is nothing less than the metaphysical verse of sentimentalism—is exactly the "point." Cowley calls for a "blended fire" of poetry and sexuality:

> The *one,* poetic language give,
> The *other* bid thy passion live;

Later romantic writers become preoccupied with Paolo and Francesca, Launcelot and Guenevere, Tristan and Isolde, in order to explore what D. G. Rossetti would call "the difficult deeps of love." The kiss is the earliest figure of those deeps, and it focuses a great deal of Della Cruscan writing:

> The greatest bliss
> Is in a kiss—
> A kiss by love refin'd,
> When springs the soul
> Without controul,
> And blends the bliss with mind.
>
> (Charlotte Dacre ["Rosa Matilda"],
> "The Kiss," 1–6)[9]

The fact that we cannot tell whether it is the kiss or the soul that "blends the bliss with mind" underscores the radical confusions being sought in texts such as these. Abused by Gifford, these blendings execute the drama Mark Akenside called the pleasures of imagination

(1744). Coleridge's more measured "balance and reconciliation of opposite and discordant qualities" here "springs . . . without controul" because Dacre's theory of imagination stands closer to a "Prolific" Blakean "Energy" than to Coleridge's more conceptual approach to the subject.

We have to pause a bit—it isn't difficult—over this matter of kissing, for it locates an important feature of the Della Cruscan experience. Recalling the troubadours and the *stil novisti* is here once again useful. Unlike their medieval precursors, as we have seen, the *tensi* of the English Della Cruscans involved women as much as men. We mark a related difference in the importance the Della Cruscans attach to the so-called lower senses. Troubadour poetry is dominated by vision, the "highest" of the senses, the one (it was thought) closest to the mind's intellectual powers. In the sense of touch, on the other hand, we are truly imbruted, our debasement fully manifest.

Starting from Locke, however, eighteenth-century sensationalist thought revolutionized the Western imagination of the body. Without going into this large and complex subject, we can say, in the present context, that the Della Cruscan celebration of the "feeling mind" (2:26) and the "sensate heart" (2:171) institutionalized Locke's revolution. So Charlotte Dacre's poem "The Kiss" argues—*argues!*—not simply that kissing is an intellectual experience but that it *ought* to be the highest type of intellectual activity.

A brief digression—interesting, I hope, and relevant to the question of the Della Cruscans. Though kissing in one perspective—Dante's, for example, in *Inferno,* Canto V—has been made a *figura* for a (lower) sensual corruption of the highest good (Love), an even more ancient Christian tradition was able to see the kiss otherwise. Among primitive Christians what we now call the French kiss, or soul kiss, was called the kiss of peace and was widely practiced among the faithful. Through the kiss of peace Christians engaged a spiritual intercourse—the exchange of breath being meaningful not simply as a cultic sign but, more significantly, as a sacramental (i.e., outward and material) event.[10]

Della Cruscan kissing makes a secular return to that kind of imagination. The inheritance of Locke, especially as it passed through Sterne, opened doors of perception which had been shut or hidden for centuries. Eyes closed, kissing lovers enter the voluptuous rooms of a long-forgotten palace, the tactile body, at once electric and material.

Blake's work is of course preoccupied with this move to redeem the erotic corpus. It is a literal subject in *The Book of Thel* (1789), the *Songs* (1788–94), and *The Visions of the Daughters of Albion* (1793), but it appears in more cosmological forms everywhere. "The lust of the goat is the bounty of God," for (according to Blake) a certain "Metaphysics" has turned the body to a cavern, a "palace of eternity" to "the jaws of the hungry grave" (*Visions*, 6:1).[11] When Blake drives the angel before him in plates 17–19 of *The Marriage of Heaven and Hell* (1793), the event transforms a dungeon to a pastoral paradise. The underground hell of the Bible becomes a Venusberg.

Similar experiences preoccupy all romantic poets. Keats' work is especially important. When "Kisses four" take Keats' knight at arms into *his* Venusberg, he wakens not to a Blakean heaven but "the cold hillside." A nightmare imagination intervenes "To turn a palace to a tomb" ("The Giaour," 281).[12] The nightmare is ancient, Platonic, ultimately misogynist: the body, which is woman, promises heavens of pleasure, but these heavens, real enough in themselves, are also impermanent. Erotic love, grounded in the body, cannot escape the body's limitations.

Like Blake, however, the Della Cruscans escape Keats' nightmare by starting from a different imagination of the relation of pleasure and pain. The hell of Keats' Paolo and Francesca is flaw-blown by a "melancholy storm," and the darkness proceeds from the same imagination announced by Urizen when he destroyed the world:

> I have sought for a joy without pain,
> For a solid without fluctuation.
> Why will you die, O Eternals?
> Why live in unquenchable burnings?
> (*The [First] Book of Urizen*, ch. 2, v. 3)[13]

Hidden in those troubled questions are their ecstatic answers: one dies in order to love, and one enters the fiery furnace because to do so is exactly to display the triumph of eternal life.

Della Cruscan poetry dwells on these subjects repeatedly, "to a fault" in several senses. In the exchanges of Anna Matilda and Della

(37)

Friendſhip's the Wine of Life; But Friendſhip *new*   600
(Not ſuch was His) is neither Strong, nor Pure.
O! for the bright Complexion, cordial warmth,
And elevating Spirit, of a Friend,
For twenty Summers ripening by my ſide;
All Feculence of Falſhood long thrown down;
All Social Virtues riſing in his Soul;
As Cryſtal clear; and ſmiling, as they riſe!
Here Nectar flows; it ſparkles in our ſight;
Rich to the Taſte, and genuine from the Heart.
High-flavour'd Bliſs for Gods! on Earth how rare?   610
On Earth how loſt? *Philander* is no more.

Think'ſt thou the Theme intoxicates my Song?
Am I too warm? Too warm I cannot be,
I lov'd him much; but now I love him more.
Like Birds, whoſe Beauties languiſh, half conceal'd,
Till mounted on the Wing, their gloſſy Plumes
Expanded ſhine with Azure, Green, and Gold;
How Bleſſings brighten as they take their Flight?
H's

William Blake. Watercolor illustration for Edward Young's Night Thoughts.
Night Two, *lines 600–618. 1796. British Museum, London.*

William Blake. Watercolor illustration for Edward Young's Night Thoughts.
Night Eight, lines 1249–68. 1796. British Museum, London.

Crusca, the lady recurrently draws herself toward "INDIFFERENCE" because the pleasures of "SENSIBILITY," coming and going, inflame and tear her nerves. To inhabit such a world is precisely to "live in unquenchable burnings,"

> where the Sun, with downward torrid ray
> *Kills,* with the barb'rous glories of the day.
>> ("Ode to Indifference," 1:76)

The elision in "barb'rous" is telling, and a typical feature of Della Cruscan wit. Gifford deplored it as a trick of mere "letters," which is of course true enough, so far as that idea of the matter goes. Anna Matilda takes it further, picking up various motifs in the couplet (in particular "barb'rous," "torrid," and the killing Sun) and playing transformations on them:

> Oh! she has torn the slumbers from my lids:
> Oft rous'd my torpid sense to living woe,
> And bid chill anguish to my bosom grow.

While the conceptual subject is pain, and the referential experience suffering, the immediate *poetic* event signals the triumph of art over— say rather, *within* and through—its embracing limitations.

What is absolutely crucial to understand about this kind of writing is its extreme formality. Its world is figured, consciously artificial. To read it one would do well to recall one of Pound's famous "don'ts" in "A Retrospect": "When Shakespeare talks of the 'Dawn in russet man- tle clad' he presents something which the painter does not present. There is in this line of his nothing that one can call description; he presents."[14] There is in Anna Matilda's lines, in Della Cruscan writ- ing generally, nothing that one can call description. All is present-ed through and as letters. Anna Matilda's world is her text—immediate, material, self-conscious, limited to language. Her art reflects (upon) a reality imagined in a similar design.

Immersed in that textual condition, however, Anna Matilda cannot comprehend its truth. In this respect she utters words, like Blake's Urizen, whose entire meaning she cannot herself realize. So her "Ode to Indifference" is answered—really, is read and interpreted—by Della Crusca.

> O CEASE MATILDA! cease thy strain,
> That wooes INDIFFERENCE to thy arms;
> For what are all her boasted charms?
> *But only to be free from Pain!*
>
> (1:78)

Della Crusca begins to develop Anna Matilda's poetic thought—her "feeling mind," her "sensate heart"—by invoking the multiple meanings carried in the word "strain" (familial, musical, poetic, biological). Pleasure is fraught with its reciprocal pain, and Anna Matilda's expressed desire for untormented love, being itself a form of desire, generates "the LUXURY OF WOE." This is Della Crusca's phrase, however, not Anna Matilda's; that is, Della Crusca gives a local habitation and, most important, a name to Anna Matilda's style. He reveals part of its *luxurious* meaning. In doing so, he begins to establish the signs of the limits of his own imaginings. His admonition "CEASE," for example, is in an important sense the precise opposite of what he wants of her, of the truth of his true desire.

The *tenso* format is the key device for gradually unfolding more of the literal truth to the conversing writers. (Of course the *full* truth can never be disclosed, only *fore*closed—by ceasing to enter and regenerate the world of letters.) Anna Matilda first responds to, then resists, the "Poetic ardors" (2:160) aroused by Della Crusca. For his part, Della Crusca is "recalled to love" by his own impulse of renunciation, and the recall is literalized in Anna Matilda's first lyrical response. But that response builds up its own structure of internal resistances, so that a complex pattern of nested tensions gradually unfolds itself. The whole exchange comprises a dialectic of ambiguous resistances and stimulations: "flights" alternating figures of fear and of ecstasy, binding "strains" of music and tortured nerves.

A Living Theater

To Wordsworth (to return to Wordsworth), these literalists of imagination were deplorable not for having failed in their art but for having proposed such an artistic procedure in the first place. It was, in a word, insincere: a game of words rather than a true expression of true feeling. The language of poetry is not to be measured by a norm of artifice but by what Wordsworth calls the "real language of men." Poetry succeeds, for Wordsworth, to the degree that it approximates such a language, for only that "real" language can hope to express what is "permanent" and "universal" in our nature and our feelings.[15]

Of course Wordsworth skirts the problems of his position—for example, that his "real language of men" is an artificial construction of his own (certainly in his own poetry) and that it by no means comprehends the full range of the "English" language, even the English abroad in the kingdom in 1800. Furthermore—and speaking only of poetry—"sincerity" is, after all, strictly a poetic style, a rhetorical stance. Wordsworth's project, however, was to argue the need for translating that style into a moral norm for artists. (Byron, recognizing this, laid down his parody decalogue in *Don Juan* to expose the overweening presumptuousness of Wordsworth's position.) The second of the essays "Upon Epitaphs" supplies an excellent gloss on the (often recondite) argument of the *Lyrical Ballads'* "Preface": "When a man is treating an interesting subject, or one which he ought not to treat at all unless he be interested, no faults have such a killing power as those which prove that he is not in earnest, that he is acting a part. . . . This is one of the most odious of faults; because it shocks the moral sense."[16] This comment explains why Wordsworth found Della Cruscan verse so abhorrent. Love and sympathy, the relation of thought and feeling, or art and life: these are the large and "interesting" subjects addressed by the Della Cruscans. Their work is "odious" because of its theatricality, because it is "not in earnest" as Wordsworth imagines it should be.

Coleridge's views on these matters in *Biographia Literaria* are relevant and instructive.[17] Taking up the "second defect" in Wordsworth's poetry, Coleridge expands his earlier remark about the momentary "willing suspension of disbelief . . . that constitutes poetic faith" (2:6). The root of the defect Coleridge locates in Wordsworth's idea that poetry "proposes *truth* for its immediate object, instead of *pleasure*" (2:130). Wordsworth's project tries "to make [poetry] what it ought to be," that is, a form of expression in which no gaps open between *res* and *verba*. But this is to place a demand upon poetry which can only be realized when "the blessed time shall come, when truth itself shall be pleasure, and both shall be so united, as to be distinguishable in words only, not in feeling" (2:130). Coleridge is saying that poetry creates virtual worlds. This being so, the poet will only destroy the rhetorical effect of his fictions if he asks the reader to judge them by measures of truth or reality. For Coleridge, poetry works by a delicate kind of "*negative faith*": namely, the "willing suspension of *dis*belief" (my italics) in what a critical intelligence, if permitted to operate, would judge unreal, things of mere words, "letters" (as Gifford called the *unbelievable* language of the Della Cruscans).

Much closer to the Della Cruscans than Wordsworth, Coleridge came under their influence for a brief time in the early nineties, as one sees in such poems as "Kisses," "The Sigh," and "The Kiss," among others.[18] He differs from them in one crucial respect: for Coleridge, the verbal structures erected by the poet will ideally comprise symbols of a transcendental order much closer to the Wordsworthian imagination. The logical form of this symbolical relation eventually gets expressed in the theory of the primary and the secondary imaginations. The latter constructs a figural totality analogous to the primal (Judaeo-Christian) act of creation—a finished and unified form wherein various opposite and discordant qualities are balanced and reconciled.

This context of more traditional romantic thought throws the differential of the Della Cruscans into bold relief. As we have already seen, the dialectics of the Della Cruscan *tenso* do not permit the symbolist approach to writing favored by Coleridge. Furthermore, as Coleridge seeks communion with "the one Life within us and abroad," the Della Cruscans pursue change, variety, and a succession of diverse experiences. That feature of the work comes out early, in *The Florence Miscellany* (1785), the volume that brought the movement into public attention. The title is itself an index of a writing committed to change and variety. The book mixes Italian and English poets and poetry, men and (at this point only) one woman (Mrs. Piozzi). The Miltonic model of *L'Allegro / Il Penseroso* is explicitly invoked in numerous poetic pairings, the most important of which is Merry's "Il Viaggio" and "La Dimora." In the ambitious poem "Valombrosa," a culminant text in the book, Merry sets "the ardent love of change" and a "Lavish . . . maze" of experience against an "unvaried round" of existence bound by "chains of habit" (186–87): in typical Della Cruscan style, "change" versus "chains." The point is not to bring order to variety but to stimulate and provoke. Artificial reconstructions of nature everywhere spread and multiply into further textualities.

The mechanism generating these generations is the theatricality of the verse, its conscious pursuit of illusion and surface effects. Where Coleridge understands poetry to function through a suspension of critical disbelief, the Della Cruscans argue that it comes exactly from the self-conscious display of disbelieved forms and fanciful gestures. In poetry, being earnest becomes important only when one isn't.

The Della Cruscan who explores this paradox most thoroughly is William Parsons. His "Story of Francesca, from the Fifth Canto of DANTE'S INFERNO" uses the method of what Parsons calls "Free Translation" to weave his Della Cruscan interpretation into the re-worked Dantescan original. The clear differences between Dante's text and what Parsons makes of it can be seen in Francesca's famous climactic comment upon the sinful event:

> Galeotto fu il libro e chi lo scrisse:
> Quel giorno piu non vi leggemmo avante.
>
> $(137-38)^{19}$

> Thus did that cursed book, with pois'nous art,
> To us perform it's Galeotto's part;
> That day no more the luscious page we priz'd,
> For all it feign'd in us was realiz'd.
>
> (*Miscellany*, 122)

Throughout the episode Dante's text wants us to see that the lovers have been bad readers. Had they gone on reading "that day" (to the end of the story), had they even paid attention to the text they did read (rather than to each other), their sin might have been averted. Francesca here acknowledges her culpability, but Parsons—like Dante—wants us to see that she does not understand what she knows. She speaks like that figure of contemporary legend, the reader of *Werther,* who finishes the book by committing suicide.

Parsons thus extends Dante's thought most tellingly in his climactic line, which has no linguistic equivalent in the original. The line is impossible to overpraise, at least if one values economy of rich expression. It works by the simplest of devices—locating the prepositional phrase simultaneously in two syntaxes. Parsons thus adds an unexpected gloss on Dante, a comment amounting to a brief theory of poetic mimesis: the "luscious page" loses its artistic value when its artificial status is compromised. According to Parsons' reading, text works to build a "feign'd" world "in" the lovers, a significant experience they might imaginatively engage. In this case, however, the lovers don't engage an erotic text; they choose to enter its "realiz'd" equivalent.

Parsons implicitly argues that disaster looms for readers who suspend the self-consciousness ("disbelief") promoted by textual experiences, in particular poetic experiences (for example, in spontaneously overflowing texts, or "sincere" verse).

> One day we read how Lancelot's throbbing heart
> Felt the soft torments of love's piercing dart.
> Alone we were, in innocence secure,
> For till that moment all our thoughts were pure;
> But then too oft as our uplifted eyes
> Each other met, the conscious blushes rise.
>
> (122)

Like a fever, those blushes signify that her body knows more about Francesca's danger than her mind. The text marks her mind's ignorance by her (yet maintained) idea about their mutual innocence and mental purity. "The fatal crisis" plays out Francesca's culpable lack of awareness, and the text, which might have been a Vergil to Francesca, becomes instead a Galeotto:

> When as we read how first the kiss of flame,
> On fair Ginevra's smiling mouth impress'd,
> Rais'd love's wild tumults in her yielding breast;
> The youth beside me sought an equal bliss,
> With trembling lips I met his burning kiss.
>
> (122)

But texts are not to be thus abandoned and misused. These lovers have forgotten their book, have forgotten how to read. The desire to establish a real equation between textual and personal erotics means, in this text, disaster.

Parsons translates Dante as a warning against forms of reading (or writing) which seek a real equivalence between expression and feeling, between the poetic and the personal. Parsons has turned Francesca to a monitory emblem of the poetry of sincerity. His "free translation" involves an argument about the moral function of textual fictions, whose obligations to reflection and self-consciousness (style and art) stand prior to all (rhetorical) demands for expression and sincerity. One is not surprised, consequently, that Parsons typically addresses the problem of poetry through explicit or implicit analogies between poetry's virtual worlds and the illusions of the stage.

The "Song" to his coy mistress Melissa, for example (*Miscellany,* 142), functions as a kind of allegory of art. As "Melissa's voice" "outvies" the loveliest natural sounds, it becomes a figure for, and a challenge to, the "Song" itself. But Parsons moves to meet the challenge:

> Yet can I meet devoid of fear
>   The matchless splendor of her charms;
> And when she sings unmov'd can hear,
>   Nor dread the tyrant Love's alarms.
>
>   (5–8)

Reimagined, Melissa has met more than her match in Parsons' verse, as we see in that splendid—and typically Parsonian—wordplay on "unmov'd." For the "studied airs" (16) of Melissa's singing, he goes on to say, have taught Parsons to make a theater of her art.

At the outset of his song Parsons allows that Melissa's voice "outvies" the "wood-lark's melting lays." At the end, however, he compares himself to a "free bird high-pois'd in air," "sing[ing] secure" from the "downward lure" (21–24) of Melissa's dangerous art. Like any craftsperson (see the "crafty fowlers," 22), Melissa has gained her skill through "studied" work. When she sings, she is therefore "unmov'd" and in the eyes of an imaginatively aware listener may be judged "by affectation sway'd" (13). Labeled as such, as in Brechtian theater, that affectation gives up its unexpected virtue. It appears (now) the gift of art. Parsons takes the gift and sings Melissa a responsive song, wherein her "unmov'd" song turns through its "unmov'd" hearer to a kind of metasong about the freedom that art offers.

We want to see that Parsons does not romanticize either Melissa or the art she teaches and practices. The labels "affectation" and "studied" and "fantastic" all carry their negative overtones through the text. By the same token, Parsons doesn't want to diminish her achievement, as his own song plainly indicates. If there is a grace beyond the reach of art—something this song suggests in its critique of Melissa—we can *know* its absent presence only through the measure of art: that is one of the key ideas promoted in work of this kind.

The "romantic" poems of the Della Cruscans—I have in mind significant works such as Merry's "Madness" and "Sir Roland: A Fragment"—always come labeled as such. In this respect they are literally "theatrical" works; they call attention to themselves as artistic constructs. They make one remember Charles Lamb's acute displeasure when Coleridge changed the title of the 1798 "Rime of the Ancyent Marinere" to the 1800 "Ancient Mariner: A Poet's Reverie": "It is as bad as Bottom the Weaver's declaration that he is not a lion, but only the scenical representation of a lion. What new idea is gained by this title but one subversive of all credit—which the tale should force upon us—of its truth."[20] Coleridge's change is a move in the direction of Della Cruscan self-consciousness. The "new idea . . . gained" by the revision is precisely an *idea* rather than an affect. It introduces an intellectual element into the work. Nor is this to suggest—pace *Lamb*—that the affective order of Coleridge's verse does not undergo a similarly decisive change. Bottom's declaration of his role-playing is not "bad"; it is a gesture bringing pleasures of awareness to the audience's experience. Not many would prefer Lamb's version of *A Midsummer Night's Dream* to Shakespeare's. Not many wouldn't think the original a far richer work, both intellectually and affectively.

NOTES

1. My texts from Gifford are taken from *The Baviad and Maeviad,* 6th ed. (London, 1800). Line numbers are cited parenthetically in the text.

2. See *Lyrical Ballads: Wordsworth and Coleridge,* ed. R. L. Brett and A. R. Jones (London: Methuen, 1965, new and rev. impression), 244–46, 248–50.

3. The first passage is from *William Wordsworth: The Poems,* 2 vols., ed. John O. Hayden (Harmondsworth: Penguin Books, 1977). All references to Wordsworth's poems are from this volume. Merry's passage is from *The British*

Album, 2 vols. (London, 1790). The notoriety of Della Cruscan verse was largely a consequence of these volumes, in which the amatory exchanges of Della Crusca and Anna Matilda, reprinted from Bell's periodical *The World,* were first anthologized. Citations hereafter are given in the text by volume and page number.

4. Several of William Parsons' contributions to *The Florence Miscellany* (Florence, privately printed, 1785), the movement's first important publication, explicitly address this topic of nature as imaginative reconstruction. See, for example, "On the Pleasures of Poetry," 134–36, especially stanzas 8 and 13–14. Subsequent references to the *Miscellany* are cited parenthetically in the text.

5. See note 15 below.

6. See, for example, Arley's "Elegy on the Death of Mr. Sterne" (*British Album,* 2:88–90); but Sterne is echoed and glanced at throughout Della Cruscan verse.

7. For Byron's relation to the tradition, see my essays " 'My Brain Is Feminine': Byron and the Poetry of Deception," in *Byron: Augustan and Romantic,* ed. Andrew Rutherford (London: Macmillan, 1990), 26–51, and "Byron and the Lyric of Sensibility," *European Romantic Review* (forthcoming). The relation of Moore, Shelley, and Keats to the same tradition was a continual theme of nineteenth-century literary commentary. Moore's soft pornography eventually fell completely out of favor, but the continued popularity of the other late romantics led the twentieth-century modernists to make their sentimentalism a continual object of attack.

8. Della Crusca's footnote to the passage is explicit: "This alludes to the idea of the Nightingale being enamoured of the Rose, so frequently expressed in Persian poetry"

9. Printed in Dacre's *Hours of Solitude* (London, 1805).

10. See Nicholas James Perella, *The Kiss Sacred and Profane* (Berkeley and Los Angeles: University of California Press, 1969), 20–28.

11. Quoted from *The Complete Poetry and Prose of William Blake,* ed. David V. Erdman, commentary by Harold Bloom, new and revised edition (Berkeley and Los Angeles: University of California Press, 1982).

12. Quoted from *The Poems of John Keats,* ed. Jack Stillinger (Cambridge: Harvard University Press, 1978).

13. Quoted from Erdman, ed., *Poetry and Prose of William Blake.*

14. Printed in Pound's *Pavannes and Divisions* (New York: Alfred A. Knopf, 1918).

15. For a good contextual treatment of sincerity, see Leon Guillamet, *The Sincere Ideal: Studies in Sincerity in Eighteenth-Century English Literature* (Montreal: McGill-Queens University Press, 1974).

16. See *William Wordsworth: The Literary Criticism,* ed. Paul M. Zall (Lincoln: University of Nebraska Press, 1966), 107.

17. I quote from the two-volume edition (edited by James Engell and W. Jackson Bate) in *The Collected Works of Samuel Taylor Coleridge,* Bollingen Series 75 (Princeton: Princeton University Press, 1983); citations are in the text.

18. These are all explicitly Della Cruscan works, but in 1791–94—the heyday of the Della Cruscan movement—Coleridge cultivated a style of extreme sensibility.

19. *Dante Alighieri. The Divine Comedy. Inferno 1. Italian Text and Translation,* trans. and ed. Charles Singleton, Bollingen Series 80 (Princeton: Princeton University Press, 1970).

20. See Lamb's letter to Wordsworth of January 1801, quoted in Brett and Jones, *Lyrical Ballads,* 277.

1890s, 1990s

Fin-de-Siècle Lyric: W. B. Yeats and Jorie Graham

Helen Vendler

> *The recent past always presents itself as if destroyed by catastrophe.*
>> Theodor Adorno, *Minima Moralia,* "Dwarf Fruit"

> *Except for us,*
> *The total past felt nothing when destroyed.*
>> Wallace Stevens, *Esthétique du Mal*

> *Egypt and Greece, good-bye, and good-bye Rome!*
>> W. B. Yeats, "Meru"

> *She's deep into the lateness now.*
>> Jorie Graham, "History"

*F*IN-DE-SIÈCLE writing suggests seriousness and flamboyance, hyperbole and arbitrariness. The notion of fin de siècle presents itself to reflection as unsuitable for lyric, since it derives from the time span of epic narration, and lyric generically prefers the moment to the narrative span. The primary formal problem for the writer of lyric who wishes to invoke the notion of history is to tuck such a panoramic concept into a short-breathed poem, and the fin-de-siècle poem is a subgenre within a lyric genre we could call the history poem. In this chapter I have a few words to say about the way Yeats and Graham each work toward solutions of the formal problem of reconciling the epic subject of history with the lyric moment.

But first I want to mention the literary-historical problem of the fin de siècle as a descriptive phrase. The phrase *fin de siècle,* as we have inherited it today, carries a nineteenth-century tonality, embracing a group of etiolated or exaggerated images and an associated aura of exhausted male sexuality, a sexuality replaced with the aggression of femmes fatales and a congeries of "perversions"—sadomasochism, suicide, homosexuality, incest, and so on. It would be a mistake, surely, to transfer this literary description, deriving from the nineteenth century, to the twentieth-century fin de siècle, which has already begun, as I point out with respect to Jorie Graham's work, to acquire a different, if equally disturbing, sense of itself while not distancing itself altogether from the melodrama of the nineteenth-century phase.

Even in a turn-of-the-century predecessor, the nineteenth-century classic sense of the fin de siècle can suffer revision, and I therefore begin with Yeats, who produced classic fin-de-siècle poems at the turn of the century and then rewrote them vigorously in works composed later, during the interwar period, when he saw approaching what he regarded as the end of the European cultural synthesis.

Yeats thought about the fin de siècle in four ways, derived from theories of history—classical, Christian, Celtic, and Nietzschean— available to him. Between 1889 and 1899, he saw the end of the century principally, as I've mentioned, in terms we are accustomed to think characteristic of the nineteenth-century fin de siècle—weariness, exhaustion, enervation. These are qualities a young man delights to express as, for the first time, he represents experience to himself as repetitive, too thoroughly known, too exhaustively foreseeable. In *The Wanderings of Oisin* (1889), Yeats' account of the kidnapping of the passive hero by a fairy femme fatale, the decadent tones that we associate with the French and British fin de siècle are thoroughly explored, and the subsequent volume *The Wind among the Reeds* (1899), with its poems of hopeless yearning, expressed in the dying fall of uncertain and quavering rhythms, is the fin-de-siècle book par excellence. It is in *The Wind among the Reeds* that we can begin to chart Yeats' conceptual models of the fin de siècle.

The Christian apocalyptic tradition is visible in the 1899 poem "The Secret Rose":

> When shall the stars be blown about the sky
> Like the sparks blown out of a smithy, and die?
> Surely thine hour has come, thy great wind blows,
> Far-off, most secret, and inviolate Rose?[1]

Considered formally, "The Secret Rose" acts to compress epic time into lyric time by allusion to three of four events assumed to be well known; these take us from the archaic period through to the present. But Yeats is already drawn to another model of the end, a more political one, as he writes a poem about the Celtic Armageddon, the battle in the Valley of the Black Pig, on which his note reads: "All over Ireland there are prophecies of the coming rout of the enemies of Ireland, in a certain Valley of the Black Pig, and these prophecies are, no doubt, now, as they were in the Fenian days, a political force" (449). The entropic model of weariness unto death, the Blake-derived model of the Christian Apocalypse, and the political model of the great battle all present themselves to Yeats as plausible imaginative schemes for lyric at the turn of the century. But at this time, his tone does not change perceptibly from one model to the other. His tone does finally change in the twenties once he has encountered the ideas of Nietzsche and Spengler; he now begins to rewrite his earlier poems, as he takes on his favorite model by far of the fin de siècle, that of the repetitive but innovative spiral or gyre or vortex.

As "gyres run on" (343), subjective and objective eras succeed each other; Yeats' model for these is the classical era succeeded by the Christian era. At the end of the Christian era, expected in the year A.D. 2000, a new subjective era will, he announces, arrive; it will have as its dominating symbol not Helen of Troy, the child who inaugurated the two-thousand-year classical era before Christ, but the Rough Beast, who now replaces Jesus in the manger:

Now I know
That twenty centuries of stony sleep
Were vexed to nightmare by a rocking cradle,
And what rough beast, its hour come round at last,
Slouches towards Bethlehem to be born?

(185)

Though "The Second Coming" was not written at a calendric fin de siècle, it was written at the end of an era, when the First World War had destroyed Europe's peace and the Easter rising, followed by the Troubles and a civil war, had changed the governance of Ireland. Yeats certainly believed that he was witnessing the breakup of the Christian historical era, as he says in *A Vision* (his conspectus of "history"); and in such poems as "The Second Coming" and "Leda and the Swan" he was in fact rewriting his early 1899 fin-de-siècle poems in a new imaginative form, as anticipatory fin-de-siècle poems characterizing the year 1999.

Yeats had also come to realize the inutility of statement in verse without a corresponding authenticating form, and both "The Second Coming" and "Leda and the Swan" find new formal models for the fin de siècle. "The Second Coming"—to resume it briefly in formal terms—is written in two unrhymed parts. The first contains eight lines and is written in an impersonal mode—"Things fall apart, the centre cannot hold"; the second contains fourteen lines and is written in the first person—"The darkness drops again, but now *I know*." We may interpret this doubled form as an attempt, in the first eight lines, to write an octave of impersonal "public" political discourse which has aspirations—visible in its eight-line exposition of a "problem"—toward the sonnet form. But the generalizing octave fails and cannot find its sestet. The writer then decides to rewrite his public and impersonal octave in a personal and lyric voice and is rewarded for his turn to lyric authenticity by a "vision out of Spiritus Mundi" in which he sees the awakening of the Rough Beast. His second attempt at a sonnet succeeds in providing both a consolidating image (in its Rough Beast "octave," which actually spills over, in a Miltonic *volta*, into the ninth line) and an intellectual conclusion—"Now I know." However, this successful "sonnet" still retains the blank-verse form as a signal of its wish to speak in the unrhymed lines of the initial failed octave. Blank verse is the lyric convention for speech or public oratory, whereas rhymed lines are the lyric convention for song. An originary failed speech—which yet has aspirations toward lyric vision—is "replaced" by a sonnet, which yet, by keeping its oratorical aim (as shown by its unrhymed lines), deflects sonnet writing away from private song.

Similarly, in "Leda and the Swan," the formal model for "the cycle of the solid having turned"—Wallace Stevens' phrase—is the gradual metamorphosis of Zeus from pure bird (wings, bill, dark webs) to God (a glory and a rush) to human lover (a breast, a beating heart) to a synthesis of all three ("the brute [bird] blood [lover] of the air [sky-god]") before he returns to being pure bird (an "indifferent beak," 212). In these two poems, "The Second Coming" and "Leda and the Swan," Yeats folds epic into lyric by forcing the fin-de-siècle double moment, which combines cultural catastrophe with inception, to stand, by synecdoche, for the whole epic and dramatic narration it engenders:

> A shudder in the loins engenders there
> The burning wall, the broken roof and tower
> And Agamemnon dead.
>
> (212)

However, Yeats was too shrewd a poet not to suspect that beyond those models of time which he used to posit a sharp breaking point— the Apocalypse, the battle in the Valley of the Black Pig, the impregnation of Leda by Zeus—there might be another model of history, a model of "plus ça change," or (as Shakespeare said in sonnet 59) "whether revolution be the same." What if one stood outside the turns of history and merely watched, instead of being a participant? In certain poems written just before the outbreak of World War II, such as "Meru" and "Lapis Lazuli," Yeats imagines detached spectators (they are always Asian—Himalayan monks in "Meru," "three Chinamen" in "Lapis Lazuli") who can watch the decay of the West without chagrin.

These Asian contemplatives have now succeeded their "Christian" predecessors the Magi, who, in Yeats' World War I poem called "The Magi," watch without contentment or satisfaction a repeated historical panorama of Christ's life. Unsatisfied by the ignominy and mystery of

Bethlehem, the Magi remain to watch for the outcome they expect, the triumphant coming of the Messiah; instead they find the greater fin-de-siècle confusion of Calvary. The Magi remain, therefore, in Yeats' imagination, figures for those who know that every worked-up emotion welcoming a fin de siècle is a fraud, that repetitiveness is the only truth:

> Now as at all times I can see in the mind's eye,
> In their stiff, painted clothes, the pale unsatisfied ones
> Appear and disappear in the blue depth of the sky
> With all their ancient faces like rain-beaten stones,
> And all their helms of silver hovering side by side,
> And all their eyes still fixed, hoping to find once more,
> Being by Calvary's turbulence unsatisfied,
> The uncontrollable mystery on the bestial floor.
>
> (124)

Unlike Yeats' later hermits and Chinese sages, the Magi have no capacity for tragic joy: they follow the gyres perpetually unsatisfied. They stand for the participant in history who is convinced that history is repetition without any ultimate meaning. Yeats emphasizes in this poem not simply inception—as the later Leda and Rough Beast poems do, while envisaging an end as well—but *both* poles, inception and conclusion. By writing "The Magi" in the hexameters that are the formal sign of epic, he gestures toward the whole Christian epic, which is contained in the Magi's ceaseless circling. In this bleak picture of history—especially bleak because it is predicated of the Magian witnesses to Christian incarnation and redemption—Yeats indulges his suspicion that the Magi can put no construction on divine history which will satisfy their quest for epic intelligibility.

Nonetheless, in spite of its cognitive dismay, "The Magi" is written with a formal repetitiveness that stands in for meaning. Repetitiveness itself becomes meaning because it is predictable: it precludes the random. The story of Jesus has only two poles, Bethlehem and Calvary, and we see their inexorable and predictable return—or rather the Magi's return to each of them in succession. If history is meaningless, it is at least predictable. In his later suspicion that his desired "tragic joy" was available only to nonparticipants in a given cycle, Yeats concedes the power, for participants in history, of any model of meaning—the circular classical passage from Golden Age to Iron Age and back, the linear Christian passage from Creation to Apocalypse, or the political rise from defeat to victory in the Valley of the Black Pig. These models, as I have said, like the model of repetitiveness, all find formal equivalents in Yeats' poetry. What does not find a formal equivalent in his practice, because Yeats did not entertain it conceptually, is randomness. He could tolerate the cognitive dissonance among his models of history because all of them rested on a notion of the predictable—demonstrated, in all his models, thematic and formal, by his patterned dynamic and his metrical order.

WHAT INTERESTS me in Jorie Graham's recent work on models of history is that she avoids not only the classical and Christian models invoked by Yeats and others but also the utopian models invoked by socialist and feminist poets. Instead, like Ashbery, whose favorite image of life is a ride on a circling carrousel with no destination, Graham attempts to be in the flow before demarcating it, though she also ponders demarcation. The continuum of history—rather than the events that demarcate and thereby organize time—is her subject. The continuum resists being called the *fin* of anything. And yet ends—or at least significant events—keep happening in Graham's poems; this is not usually the case in Ashbery, who tends, with his theoretical commitment to irony, to will "events" as such into one single level of pleasant insignificance.

Jorie Graham is now in her early forties, not far from Yeats' age as the last century turned; the absence in her work of the world-weariness of his in the nineties suggests that what we are accustomed to call a fin-de-siècle tone—blanched, pale, sighing—is a limited phenomenon derived from certain poems of Swinburne, the Rossettis, and Yeats, themselves reacting against strenuous and even bombastic romantic and Victorian tonalities of revolution and moral endeavor. This reaction against revolutionary bombast and utopian conviction (with their concurrent preachiness) may have only coincidentally arrived at the end of the last century, and our fin de siècle, as the twentieth century draws to a close, promises to have, whether in novels such as Don DeLillo's *Mao II* or in poetry such as Graham's, a tone of its own—confused rather than weary, screen-mobile rather than painting-static, jump-cut rather than continuous, interrogative rather than de-clarative, and ambiguous rather than conclusive. The conviction that one can speak authentically only of personal experience (in *Mao II*, that of the writer and photographer, for instance) and an equal convic-tion that one must speak also of incomprehensible mass events (in *Mao II*, the Moonie mass marriage) struggle for dominance at this historical moment. Mass synecdoche, if one may call it that, is the substitute for the nineties' synecdoche of the detail. And yet the falsification of anything in representing it as a group phenomenon causes the com-pensatory insistence on the private. The formal incoherence caused in a recent novel such as *Mao II* by authorial insistence—without nineteenth-century ligatures of plot coherence—on a simultaneity of mass and private phenomena offers textual evidence of the imaginative strain involved in such witnessing.

Graham's preoccupation with history and the end of history appears in marked form in several poems found in her 1991 book *Region of Unlikeness*.[2] The poems I have in mind reveal, even in their titles, Graham's intent to reflect on significant event, the temporal contin-uum, the forms of narrative, and the competitive roles of participant and watcher. The poems in question have as titles "History" (two poems are given that title), "Act III, Sc. 2," "Who Watches from the Dark Porch," and "The Phase after History." Graham's foreword to *Region of Unlikeness* quotes Augustine in the *Confessions,* as he broods on language as successivity and the human wish to spatialize that suc-cessivity: "You hear what we speak . . . and you do not want the syllables to stand where they are; rather you want them to fly away so that others may come and you may hear a whole sentence. So it is with all things that make up a whole by the succession of parts; such a whole would please us much more if all the parts could be perceived at once rather than in succession" (xi). In the poem called "Act II, Sc. 2," Graham spatializes her own life into textual form, significantly not choosing, as Yeats would have, the moment of inception or conclusion but rather borrowing from Stevens an intermediate moment in the epic drama. (The poem of Stevens from which she borrows is one called "Chaos in Motion and Not in Motion," in which Stevens first names the moment in time, "Chaos in Motion," and then in textual space, "and not in Motion." In it, he announces that at this late moment "Scene 10 becomes 11, / In Series X, Act IV, et cetera.")[3] Graham's theme in "Act II, Sc. 2" is the problem of representing accurately one's position in participatory terms once one has begun, in middle life, to be a watcher of one's own history even as one enacts it:

> Look she said this is not the distance
> we wanted to stay at—We wanted to get
> close, very close. But what
> is the way in again? And is it
>
> too late? She could hear the actions
> rushing past—but they are on
> another track.
>
> (66)

Many of Graham's poems enact a rapid zooming, in alternately long and short lines, between getting close and gaining distance; this poses a problem of historical representation at all times. But a preoccupation with the degree to which the events of history are mentally and textually constructed into acts and scenes rather than "objectively" recorded is what differentiates contemporary historiographers and poets of the fin de siècle from those who, like Spengler and Yeats, tended to accept constructions already invented, even if such schemes—linear, circular, spiral shaped—were inconsistent with one another. As Stevens said of the mind in "Of Modern Poetry":

> It has not always had
> To find: the scene was set; it repeated what
> Was in the script. Then the theatre was changed
> To something else. Its past was a souvenir.[4]

In Graham's recent poetry, time itself and the recorder of time are intimately linked, cannot be conceptually separated, in that it is only the recorder who demarcates time, points out moments worth remembrance. All the other moments in the continuum will sink unnoticed. How do we explain what gets recorded? Perhaps attention is random: people might record what they happened to witness or happened to come across. But Graham will not entertain that possibility: it is, for her, the sacred obligation of the recorder to pay attention at the precisely fated moment:

> the only
> right time, the intended time,
> punctual,
> the millisecond I was bred to look up into, click, no
> half-tone, no orchard of
> possibilities,
>
> up into the eyes of my own
> fate not the world's.
>
> (93)

Graham's formulation here reflects the biblical idea of *kairos*, the time intended by God—usually a brief time—for some aspect of his will to become fulfilled (see, e.g., Romans 13:11, "Knowing the time . . . now it is high time to awake out of sleep"; or I Corinthians 4:5, "Therefore judge nothing before the time, until the Lord come, who both will bring to light the hidden things of darkness, and will make manifest the counsels of the hearts").

As she says in this passage, Graham also believes, in opposition to many historical poets, that it is only by chronicling accurately and punctually one's individual fate that one can, in lyric, "do" history. Against Yeats' prophetic wish to describe the world's fate as well as his own, Graham records the world's fate through her own. She can write about the epic of the Holocaust only by filtering it through the memory of a childhood visit to her Jewish grandmother confined to a nursing home. In this way, Graham sets herself against the purely spectatorial perspective of Yeats' Chinamen or Himalayan hermits and against the conventionally generalized prophetic position of contemporary poets such as Rich, who often write about broad social conditions without explicit autobiographical reference to their own motivation within, or limits with respect to, the social problem at hand.

Attention, says Graham in the second poem she entitles "History," is always processing time; but Attention, gnawing the minutes like Ovid's *tempus edax* (Shakespeare's "Devouring Time"), is not, she argues, as we might think, free ranging, but chained. Historical attention, which Graham in the following passage calls "x," is always chained, at least for the poet, by private vocation:

> Listen:
> the x gnaws, making stories like small smacking
>
> sounds,
>   whole long stories which are its gentle gnawing.
> .   .   .   .
>   If the x is on a chain, licking its bone,
>
> making the sounds now of monks
>   copying the texts out,
> muttering to themselves,
>   if it is on a chain
> .   .   .   .
>
> that hisses as it moves with the moving x,
>   link by link with the turning x
> (the gnawing now Europe burning)
>   (the delicate chewing where the atom splits),
> if it is on a chain—
>   even this beast—even this the favorite beast—
> then this is the chain, the gleaming
>
>   chain: that what I wanted was to have looked up at
>   the right
> time,
>   to see what I was meant to see,
> to be pried up out of my immortal soul,
>   up, into the sizzling quick—
>
> That what I wanted was to have looked up at the only
>   right time, the intended time,
> punctual,
>   the millisecond I was bred to look up into.
>   (92–93)

Reflection on history is peculiarly intensified by the arrival of the fin de siècle—"she's deep into the lateness now" (35), says Graham's first "History"—because of the arbitrary and relatively recent nature of century demarcation. One wants to characterize the departing century and to anticipate the new one, while conscious of the fictional and ultimately textual nature of such characterizations. The worst—or best—fin-de-siècle speculation is the apocalyptic one: that this is the absolute end of time, that there will be no more history. If the Christian Apocalypse, where all shall be revealed and justice shall be made manifest, is the sublimely comic version of the end of history, for Graham, Shakespearean tragedy, with its final obliteration of the central dramatis personae, is the atheist and materialist version of the end of history. In her extraordinary poem "The Phase after History," Graham brings together, in her characteristic way of coping with simultaneity, three narratives—linked as natural event, autobiographical experience, and literary archetype. The first narrative, of natural event, is that of an incident in which a bird has become lost in Graham's house and is about to batter itself to death against a windowpane unless she can find it and release it. The second narrative, that of autobiographical experience, retells the attempted suicide (followed by a successful suicide) of one of Graham's young students, who attempted with a knife to carve his face away from his body. The third narrative, representing the archetype behind both anterior narratives, is drawn from *Macbeth,* in which an old order, represented by Duncan, is brought to an end by Lady Macbeth in order to begin, as she hopes, a new phase of history, the dynastic reign of the Macbeths over Scotland. In the person of Lady Macbeth, Graham represents the fin de siècle as an active moment of assassination, in which the poet must kill the old century and the future it envisioned—Duncan and Duncan's sons—in order to begin a new era. The guilt and self-murder entailed are fully acted out in Graham's horrifying "phase after history."

For Graham, the human face symbolizes the forward-pointing, future-envisioning part of the self. One's normal tenderness toward one's own envisaged future is sharply checked by a self-hatred that causes either suicide or self-revision. One is convinced that for oneself there must come about a moment of decisive change, a fin de siècle, that whatever follows must be different. An attempt to hear in one's inner being the rustle of a hitherto unenvisaged future—the bird's attempt to find a way out of the house—produces whatever meaning can be extracted from the fin de siècle:

> Which America is it in?
> Which America are we in here?
> Is there an America comprised wholly
> of its waiting and my waiting and all forms of the thing
>
> . . . .
>
> a place of *attention?*
>
> (114)

Most of the notions of the future which first occur to the mind are false, trivial, wrong, incomplete, exhausted, inadequate. The Muse, rejecting these, tells the poet to wait until the right sentence of art, Keats' unheard melody, Graham's "inaudible . . . utterance," formulates itself:

> The voice says wait. Taking a lot of words.
> The voice always says wait.
> The sentence like a tongue
> in a higher mouth
>
> to make the other utterance, the inaudible one,
> possible,
> the sentence in its hole, its cavity
> of listening,
> flapping, half dead on the wing, through the
> hollow indoors,
> the house like a head
> with nothing inside
> except this breeze—
> shall we keep going?
> where is it, in the century clicking by?
> Where, in the America that *exists?*
>
> (114)

It is at this point in "The Phase after History" that Shakespeare enters: we hear a version of the voice of Duncan in *Macbeth,* wholly wrong about the future, as he says, arriving at the castle where he will be murdered, "This castle hath a pleasant seat, . . . the air nimbly recommends itself." The play makes it clear that Duncan's subsequent use of the word *guest* refers to "the temple-haunting martlet"; Graham, trusting us to remember the baffled bird flying crazily through her house, continues in an ironic misquotation, thinking of both the deceived Duncan and the endangered bird, "the guest approves / by his beloved mansionry [for "loved masonry"] / that heaven's breath smells wooingly here" (115).

Thus ends part 1 of "The Phase after History." Part 2 begins, "The police came and got Stuart, brought him to / Psych Hospital. / The face on him the face he'd tried to cut off" (116). The voice of Shakespeare, now as Lady Macbeth, reenters, saying in altered words, of the student, not of Duncan, "Who would have imagined a face / could be so full of blood" (116). Stuart's future suicide is seen as a flash-forward in the past tense: "Later he had to take the whole body off // to get the face" (118). Stuart in the hospital, between attempted suicide and subsequent successful suicide, becomes the terrified bird unable to imagine its own future, as the poet waits

> to hear something rustle
> and get to it
> before it rammed its lights out
> aiming for the brightest spot, the only clue.
>   (118)

The end of this fin-de-siècle poem comes in a flutter of inability to kill the old order or, if the old is killed, to bring to birth the new. We cannot truly see "the phase after history." The poet becomes Lady Macbeth, not knowing whether the bird–sentence–face–old order is alive or dead and, if dead, how to cleanse one's hands of the deed of murder:

> (make my keen knife see not the
> wound it makes)—
>
> . . . .
>
> Is the house empty?
> Is the emptiness housed?
> Where is America here from the landing, my face on

my knees, eyes closed to hear
　　further?
Lady M. is the intermediary phase.
　　God help us.
Unsexed unmanned.
　　Her open hand like a verb slowly descending onto
the free,

her open hand fluttering all round her face now,
　　trying to still her gaze, to snag it on

those white hands waving and diving
　　in the water that is not there.

(120–21)

It is the most hopeless ending in Graham, in effect ending the
tragedy with the suicidal Lady Macbeth. It refuses the Shakespearean
pseudoconsolation of the restoration of the anterior old order in the
crowning of Duncan's son Malcolm. In this way, Graham remains
faithful to the imaginative truth of Shakespeare's play, which is interested in the fate of the Macbeths rather than of the Duncan dynasty.
For Graham here, the fin de siècle lies suspended in Lady Macbeth's
fluttering hand, unable to still her dreaming gaze, helpless to find the
absolving water. If history is a construction, then nothing guarantees
its future except the restless and unstillable flux of the human gaze,
suicidal in its metaphysical uncertainty and in its determination to
annihilate its own past.

We may pause a moment to deduce, from this poem, that Graham
thinks any account of "the phase after history" incomplete without
some reference to her three simultaneities—natural event, personal
complicity, and archetypal literary patterning. Her jump cuts among
these, and especially her concern with middleness rather than with
inception, conclusion, or repetition, suggest that the fin de siècle, as we
now imagine it, is something we actively will—as Graham's student
willed his suicide—in an attempt to shake off an irredeemable past; or
that it is something we hesitate over—like Lady Macbeth in her dream
reprise of the murder—as we seek to find something to justify our
murder of the past, as we try to coordinate our executive hand and our

intentional gaze; or that it is something that we head blindly into—like the bird crashing into the invisible windowpane. The indeterminacy of these possibilities, and the poet's incapacity to decide among them, leave Graham as watcher but also, in the end (in the person of Lady Macbeth), as participant in a history she does not understand.

Another poem from *Region of Unlikeness,* one explicitly about the construction of historical event, is called "Who Watches from the Dark Porch." The watcher hears a nearby ambiguous child-cry—is it laughter? is it pain?—and must try to interpret it as a signal of the nature of being. Is Nature—or, as Graham calls it in this poem, "Matter"—inherently comic or tragic? Interpretation, appearing here allegorically personified as the consort of Matter, is necessarily tragic because mortal. Here is the beginning of "Who Watches," asking why we feel sure that our previous attempts to codify our history were lies:

> Is it because of history or is it because of matter,
> mother Matter—the opposite of In-
>   terpretation: his consort: (his purple body lies
> shattered against terrible
>   reefs)—matter, (in it
> a shriek or is it
>   laughter)
> (a mist or is it an angel they strangle)—
>   that we feel so sure we lied?
>
>   (97)

The "instant replay" of interpretation arouses a nostalgia for presence:

> Said Moses show me Your face.
>   Not the voice-over, not
> the sound track (thou shalt not thou
>   shalt not), not the interpretation—buzz—the face.
> But what can we do?
>
>   (106)

Graham ends this typical flurry of injunctions, questions, and parenthetical interjections—so different from Yeats' agitated but dominating declarativeness—with the injunction to sit still, a command borrowed from Eliot's "Ash Wednesday" but lacking Eliot's Christian implication. Both the writer's desire for revelation (which can lead to a false willed meaning) and the nostalgia for presence (which can lead to religious sentimentality) threaten the artist of the fin de siècle. Yielding to the first will create another abstract utopia of the sort the twentieth century has already seen too many of; yielding to the second will offer a premature ontology and a premature sentimental ethics.

> . . . sit still sit still the lively understandable
> spirit said,
> still, still,
> so that it can be completely the
>
> now.
>
> (108)

If this sitting—"don't wait, just sit, sit" (108)—reveals only that one is at "*the scene of the accident*" (107) and that one can only face the "pileup of erasures—play, reverse play" (107) in the scene of writing, then this will have to be the poetics exacted by Graham's disbelief, within this "lateness," in predetermined schemes of history, those schemes that have given us, in fact, the very model of the fin de siècle which Graham must, aware of the approaching fin de siècle, refuse. The Yeatsian curtain is not lifted, but then the Yeatsian darkness does not drop, either. Play, reverse play, instant replay, erase, play again—this model makes every moment both a beginning and an end. The tape runs both ways and is always provisional, always expressed, formally speaking, in the cresting and troughing irregularities of Graham's prosody. Or, in another of Graham's Yeatsian metaphors, the dice are "being incessantly retossed" (107).

Where, then, does the poet obtain confidence in representation? Her confidence, expressed in the poem "Soul Says," lies finally in the idiom of presentness itself, in the simplicity with which we say, without thinking, "The river *glints*," or "The mother *opens the tablecloth up into the wind.*" These sentences make a text, or fabric, which descends over the earth for a moment in an "alphabet of ripenesses, / what is, what could have been." Graham concludes, as Wordsworth concluded long ago, that the verbal object, insofar as it persists, becomes a natural part of the material world: "(This is a form of matter of matter she sang)" (125). As history becomes text, it is spatialized into fabric, a tarpaulin (as Ashbery called it in the poem of that name) spread to cover the perceptual field. This is, in the end, a comic resolution, by which the temporal wave of presentness causes the hilarity of articulated expression in song. The last words in *Region of Unlikeness,* closing "Soul Says," are to be thought of, we are told, as words spoken by Prospero as he lays down his art:

> Now then, I said, I go to meet that which I liken to
> (even though the wave break and drown me in laughter)
> the wave breaking, the wave drowning me in laughter—
> .   (125)

Matters of such gravity as how to demarcate time are not solved, of course, in lyric; they are merely reimagined. Graham's drowning wave (tragedy) cannot be Yeatsianly demarcated into epical inception, event, conclusion, or even into repetition; it can only be redescribed as comedy—an annihilating cosmic laughter. *The Tempest,* the single Shakespearean play that observes the unities of time, space, and action, chooses to describe the coextension of space, time, and human will as, finally, a comic form. Each only ends when all are ended, and the end of textuality and the end of history become, in *The Tempest* and "Soul Says," the comic ending of the dramaticized world. While present event and textuality—the forms of lyric—persist, there can be, Graham's work suggests, no conclusive fin de siècle; but the strain of remaining in the now of the song cannot be entirely obliterated. The song is the place, Graham writes in "Soul Says," "(Where the hurry [of time] is stopped) (and held) (but not extinguished) (no)" (125). Each of these parentheses inserted in the soul's claim is a small fin de siècle in itself.

NOTES

1. W. B. Yeats, *Collected Poems* (New York: Macmillan, 1956), 67. Page numbers for all subsequent quotations from Yeats refer to this volume and are cited parenthetically.

2. Jorie Graham, *Region of Unlikeness* (New York: Ecco Press, 1991). Page numbers for all subsequent quotations from Graham refer to this volume and are cited parenthetically.

3. Wallace Stevens, *The Collected Poems* (New York: Knopf, 1954), 357.

4. Ibid., 239.

Contributors

Leo Braudy is Bing Professor of English at the University of Southern California. He has written extensively on Restoration and eighteenth-century literature, as well as twentieth-century film. His most recent books are *The Frenzy of Renown: Fame and Its History* and *Native Informant: Essays on Film, Fiction, and Popular Culture.*

Margreta de Grazia is Associate Professor of English at the University of Pennsylvania. She is the author of *Shakespeare Verbatim* and numerous essays on language, property, and textual reproduction in the Renaissance. As a Guggenheim Fellow, she is currently writing a book on periodization.

Jerome McGann is the John Stewart Bryan Professor of English at the University of Virginia. In addition to his many books on romantic poetry, he has written widely on British and American literature from the eighteenth through the twentieth century. His major current project is the complete writings and pictures of Dante Gabriel Rossetti: a Hypermedia Research Archive.

Elaine Scarry is Professor of English at Harvard University. She has written *The Body in Pain,* and is now completing a book about war and the social contract entitled "The Matter of Consent." Her essays about the way the material world resists language are collected in *Resisting Representation.*

Helen Vendler is A. Kingsley Porter University Professor at Harvard University. She is the author of books on Yeats, Stevens, Herbert, and Keats; her essays have been collected in *Part of Nature, Part of Us* and *The Music of What Happens.* She has recently completed a new book on Shakespeare's sonnets.

Library of Congress Cataloging-in-Publication Data

Fins de siècle : English poetry in 1590, 1690, 1790, 1890, 1990 /
edited by Elaine Scarry.
p.   cm. — (Parallax)
Contents:
1590s. Fin-de-siècle Renaissance England / Margreta de Grazia —
1690s. Unturning the century : the missing decade
of the 1690s / Leo Braudy —
1790s. The literal world of the English Della Cruscans / Jerome McGann —
1890s, 1990s. Fin-de-siècle lyric : W. B. Yeats and Jorie Graham /
Helen Vendler.
ISBN 0-8018-4928-4. — ISBN 0-8018-4929-2 (pbk.)
1. English poetry—History and criticism—Theory, etc.
2. Literature and history—Great Britain.   3. English poetry—Periodization.
I. Scarry, Elaine.   II. Title: English poetry in 1590, 1690, 1790, 1890, 1990.
III. Series: Parallax (Baltimore, Md.)
PR502.F56   1995
821.009—dc20   94-15399